Acclaim for Joanna Merlin's

AUDITIONING

"Joanna Merlin's excellent guide is as friendly and useful to directors as to actors during that fateful matchmaking that precedes a film, called auditioning." —James Ivory

"This is a book for all of us—every actor, every age, every stage (or screen). A dream would be to have Joanna Merlin actually by your side, walking you through the process—but the book is a good stand in. She gives us everything we need to know, and everything we do know, but forget under the pressure of nerves and anticipation." —Anna Deavere Smith

"Joanna Merlin is the best casting director I have ever worked with." —Stephen Sondheim

"After some time in Los Angeles, one feels like a product or a commodity rather than an actor. Joanna Merlin's book reminds me that I am an actor, and puts me back in touch with the craft and the process that makes it fun and exciting. The same exhilaration we feel when we perform can be distilled into the auditioning experience. At the same time the discipline and the 'nuts and bolts' of good acting are reviewed for those of us who know (but may have forgotten) and introduced to those who never knew. This book is a textbook for planning and executing consistently thorough auditions for the length of one's career, thereby maximizing one's potential for employment." —Sean Patrick Thomas

"Both the auditioner and the auditor have a great deal to learn from this valuable book. If all of us embraced it, auditioning would be as exciting as opening night."
—Mel Shapiro, Chair, UCLA Theatre Department

"*Auditioning: An Actor-Friendly Guide* is the ultimate authority for actors needing advice or reassurance for the sometimes terrifying challenge of the audition. Joanna Merlin speaks to the actor with the calmly encouraging authority of one who really knows. As an actress, a casting director and a teacher she speaks to every aspect of auditioning in ways that are both practical and inspiring. Her book is simpler, wiser and truer than many a weightier actor-training textbook. I will recommend it to my students not only as a clear guide to making the best choices personally and creatively for their audition material, its preparation, and execution, but as a bedside bible for the actor's best behavior in general. This book is much needed and acting teachers as well as actors should heed its wisdom."
—Kristin Linklater, Chair, Theatre Arts Division,
Columbia University School of the Arts

"I wish I could buy every working actor a copy of this personal and very practical book! Joanna Merlin has it just right: auditioning is acting under very special circumstances. And 'they' are as eager to find you as you are eager to show that you're the one they've been looking for. This book—needed for a long time—tells you how to go about it as a creative peer."
—Zelda Fichandler, Chair, Graduate Acting Program,
New York University

"Joanna Merlin brings her extensive experience and unique perspective to her actor-friendly guide, combining practical and enlightened information for any and all acting levels. It is easily the finest book on the subject and will be required reading for our Professional Actor Training Program (MFA) as well as our Undergraduate Acting Program (BA)."
—Kevin Cotter, Associate Professor of Theater,
Temple University

JOANNA MERLIN

Auditioning

Joanna Merlin was a recipient of the Casting Society of America's Artios Award for Outstanding Achievement in Dramatic Feature Film Casting for Bertolucci's *The Last Emperor* and for Best Musical Theatre Casting for Sondheim and Lapine's *Into the Woods*. As Harold Prince's casting director, she cast the original Broadway productions of *Follies, A Little Night Music, Sweeney Todd, Pacific Overtures,* and *Evita,* among others, and her film casting includes Michael Cimino's *Year of the Dragon* and Merchant Ivory's *Mr. and Mrs. Bridge.*

As an actor, Merlin has appeared in six Broadway productions, including *Becket,* in which she played opposite Laurence Olivier, and *Fiddler on the Roof,* in which she created the role of Tzeitel. Her film appearances include *City of Angels; Murder and murder; Two Bits; Class Action; Mystic Pizza; The Killing Fields; Fame; Baby, It's You;* and *The Ten Commandments;* and her television appearances include *Northern Exposure; Law and Order; L.A. Law; A Marriage: O'Keeffe and Stieglitz;* and *In a Child's Name.*

Joanna Merlin teaches in the Graduate Acting Program of New York University, the Actors Center in New York, and the Manhattan School of Music Professional Musical Theater Workshop. She was a student of Michael Chekhov, and has given classes, lectures, and workshops at the Michael Chekhov Studio of New York; Circle in the Square Theatre School; American Conservatory Theater; Yale University; Columbia University; SUNY Purchase College; Stella Adler Conservatory; Michael Chekhov International Workshop in Sussex, England; and at the Eugene O'Neill Memorial Theater Center, as well as Theaterforum Kreuzberg in Berlin; and the Teatro de la Abadía in Madrid. She is a cofounder of the Non-Traditional Casting Project, and is a member of the Tony Awards Nominating Committee.

Auditioning

AUDITIONING

An Actor-Friendly Guide

JOANNA MERLIN

Foreword by Harold Prince

VINTAGE BOOKS

A DIVISION OF RANDOM HOUSE, INC.

NEW YORK

FIRST VINTAGE BOOKS EDITION, MAY 2001

Copyright © 2001 by Joanna Merlin
Foreword copyright © 2001 by Harold Prince

Library of Congress Cataloging-in-Publication Data
Merlin, Joanna.
Auditioning : an actor-friendly guide / Joanna Merlin.—1st Vintage Books ed.
p.   cm.
ISBN 0-375-72537-7
1. Acting—Auditions. I. Title.
PN2071.A92 M47 2001
792'.028—dc21
00-43759

Grateful acknowledgment is made to the following for permission to
reprint previously published material:

Applause Theater Book Publishers: Scene 5 from *A Little Night Music.*
Copyright © 1991 by Applause Theatre Book Publishers. Copyright ©
1973 by Hugh Wheeler, Stephen Sondheim and Harold S. Prince.
Music and lyrics copyright © 1973 by Revelation. Music Publishing
Corp./Beautiful Music, Inc. All rights reserved. Reprinted by permis-
sion.

Columbia TriStar Television: Material from script *My Wildest Dreams.*
Copyright © by Columbia TriStar Television. Reprinted by permission.

Naomi Foner and Paramount Pictures: Scene from the screenplay *Losing Isaiah.* Reprinted by permission.

Book design by Debbie Glasserman
Author photo © Elena Seibert

www.vintagebooks.com

Printed in the United States of America
10   9

To Duff

Acknowledgments

To Michael Chekhov whose teaching and spirit continue to inspire me, to Hal Prince who had the crazy idea of hiring me as his casting director and changed my life, to Susan Smith, my agent and dear friend, to my students who taught me most of what I know, to Paul Libin who provided my first class, to Michael Miller who gave me a leg up, and to John David Wilder and Michael Jameson who made me promise to write it down a long time ago.

To my literary agent, George Nicholson, who took a chance on a first-time writer, to Diana Secker Larson, my supportive and unflappable editor, to Austin, Itamar, Margo, and Inger who were early readers, to the guest speakers in my Career Class at New York University who shared thoughts and ideas I may not have acknowledged in the text, and to the experts who contributed their insights and advice to Chapter X of this book.

And to my daughters, Julie and Rachel, who share their lives with me and fill me with unending joy and pride, to my mom who could have been a contender and was a life force for me from the beginning, to my sister, Harriet, whose love flows wide and deep, and to my divine grandsons, Noah and Jesse, who keep me young and happy, and to all the other friends, family, and colleagues who taught, encouraged, and supported me,

I extend my most grateful thanks.

Contents

——◼——

	Foreword by Harold Prince	*xiii*
	Introduction	*xix*
I.	STOP SELF-SABOTAGE: CHANGE THE ODDS!	1
II.	THE OTHER SIDE: A DEMYSTIFICATION	19
III.	ACTABLE CHOICES: BRINGING THE TEXT TO LIFE	42
IV.	APPLYING ACTABLE CHOICES	73
V.	AUDITIONING FOR THE CAMERA	96
VI.	AUDITIONING FOR MUSICALS	122
VII.	MONOLOGUES	142
VIII.	THE AUDITIONING EVENT: A PRACTICAL GUIDE	151
IX.	TIPS	186
X.	A LITTLE ADVICE FROM SOME EXPERTS	197
XI.	THE CARE AND FEEDING OF AN ACTOR	205

Foreword

BY HAROLD PRINCE

In 1947, Marlon Brando's Stanley Kowalski exploded on Broadway and method acting had its superstar. At that time, George Abbott (for whom I would work barely a year later), extremely exasperated, called his resident casting director onto the carpet to complain that he had never seen Marlon Brando—where had they hidden him? The casting director immediately went to his files and returned with a sheaf of audition dates on which Marlon Brando *had* been seen by Abbott, and rejected. Brando never considered himself a good auditioner, and that may explain the story. On the other hand, auditions at best are compromises. Good acting results from a process, a collaboration of actor and director and fellow actors and costume designers and wigmakers. Still, there has to be a way to cast a show, and unless the director has had previous experience with an actor, or wants from that actor a performance he's seen him give before, I don't know how you can avoid auditions.

Accepting that, Joanna Merlin has written a book based on her experience as both an actor and an esteemed casting director. I pride myself on first casting Joanna as a casting director. I met her when she played Tzeitel in the original production of *Fiddler on the Roof,* which I produced. We became friends, and I kept up with her appearances not only on stage but in film and on television. In those days, active producing organizations had their own in-house casting departments. I often had three musicals running in New York, and as many companies on the road, so that office adjunct was extremely busy. There were other producers as busy as I: David Merrick, Leland Hayward, Feuer and Martin, The Theater Guild, and Rodgers and Hammerstein. Each of them had a casting department of their own. But times were changing, and film companies began calling on the services of Broadway-based actors, so some of our best casting directors were lured away by bigger salaries and more glamorous assignments, which is how I came to lose one casting director and to be in the market for another.

I could have chosen from a number of experienced Broadway candidates. Instead, I decided to invent my own. But first I needed to define who that person would be, to appropriately reflect my feeling about actors. He (or she) should probably be an actor himself. He should know the New York scene. Not only the work pool, but where the most talented young people were studying, and who were the agents with taste. Someone who had networked in the community. Finally, perhaps most important, I wanted someone who loved actors. Strange as it may seem, there are just as many casting directors who don't as there are who do, and I suppose I understand that, given the exasperating circumstances surrounding employment in this business. And then, to top it all, I wanted a mother figure, so I guess "he" fast became "she." Joanna Merlin fit all those criteria. Besides, she and her husband had two small babies, so, acting, with its rehearsals and tryouts on the road, was going to be difficult for her to accommodate. I called Joanna, proposed the idea—astonished her, I believe—and she came to see me. The idea sat well, and it was the beginning of a busy decade for both of us, during which she was instrumental in introducing me to an astonishing array of talented people who have since found fame and fortune. Her taste is impeccable. In no instance can I remember her recommending anyone less than interesting for a role. When she finally moved on, it was to tackle such humongous assignments as spending a year traveling around the U.S. and the Far East casting Bertolucci's *The Last Emperor*. An impressive accomplishment. This book of hers is not the first guide to auditioning. But the last that I remember reading is almost a quarter of a century old. Times have changed.

It's no surprise that Joanna's definition of the auditioning process would concur with mine. Her love for actors, her compassion, hasn't blinded her to their foibles. In this book she addresses their strengths and their insecurities, and she acknowledges that—artistry aside—making theater is a job. A craft. Appropriately, she sets out to demystify not only the creative process, but, most particularly, the subject of this book: auditioning. Her style may be compassionate, but it's all business, which is what a life in the theater must be.

Discipline. (Show up on time. Learn the lines.) Eschew all self-indulgence. There is no relationship between what you create and emotional anarchy. This book focuses on an actor's priorities, explains intuition vis-à-vis preparation, strips away all the glamorous folderol that draws too many people to the theater. I think I knew most of what she is writing about, and probably agree with 90 percent of it. (A good percentage, believe me!) Best of all, with regard to "actable choices," (Chapter III) I learned something I'd never known. Somewhere in the body of the book, she lists 111 verbs as objectives. How damned smart—practical—of her!

Before I wrote this, Joanna invited me to suggest anything she may have overlooked; I can't. In fact, there's quite a lot that I've overlooked over the years but, selfishly, hope that preparing auditioners take seriously. I do, however, have one comment. It's probable that what follows did not make its way into her book because, strictly speaking, it isn't about auditioning. It's about something larger: creating a career. I suspect, however, that if auditioning actors heeded what I'm about to say, they and I would benefit.

It seems to me that a wider educational spectrum, greater

inquisitiveness, more information, an enhanced vocabulary, and yes, extensive travel—the list is endless—are necessary props for an actor. Regrettably, too few people today respect the foundation that information and experience provide. Each successive year, the naturally brilliant young actors whom I see care less and less about the history of the theater, recognize fewer and fewer references to playwrights (who were contemporary in my youth), to actors, designers, theater companies, the history of this art form internationally. Everyone seems to know Stanislavsky, and certainly the Studio, but how many know Meyerhold, Piscator, the Eastern traditions of Kabuki and Noh?

Acceleration—shortcuts to the prize—has reached epidemic proportions, not only in the arts but across society.

Joanna Merlin's book couldn't come at a better time.

—HAROLD PRINCE

Introduction

———————

This book is intended for those actors, young and old, who understand that acting is, at best, a hazardous profession, but who have nonetheless made a commitment to it because there is nothing else they find as interesting or engaging. I hope acting teachers will find this text useful in guiding actors through the auditioning process. And I hope the book will interest others in the field who would like to enhance their understanding of the actor's auditioning experience. But, at bottom, this is essentially a how to do it book for you, the actor.

I was at a wedding recently, and my dinner partner was a poet and a teacher. He asked me about my work. When I told him I taught auditioning, he said, "Why does an actor need to learn how to audition? Can't he just present his talent and skills, as he would if he were acting a role?" I explained the unpredictable aspects of auditioning and the creative and emotional obstacles that actors encounter in trying to present themselves. I also explained the relentless necessity to audition throughout one's entire career, for every job, from a thirty-second commercial to *King Lear*. As a person whose profession allows him to work independently, he was amazed that any actor ever survived in the profession.

I understand that for you, the actor, auditioning is the most harrowing part of your career. I can anticipate your doubts and insecurities, for they have been my own. I want to help you avoid the "hit or miss" syndrome, careening from one audition to the next, hoping for the best. I want to help you learn how to support yourself psychologically, practically, and artistically.

I have learned about auditioning from my career as an actor in theater, film, and television, and from the "other side" as a casting director in all three media. It became clear to me when I started casting that good actors often give poor auditions and that actors need a set of tools at each juncture of the auditioning process.

I studied acting for several years with Michael Chekhov, a great actor, director, and teacher, considered by Stanislavsky to be his most brilliant pupil. In my search for a simple and accessible approach to auditioning, I found that many of Chekhov's ideas could be adapted and used in preparing an audition scene. His techniques allow you to work quickly and playfully, using your intuition, senses, and imagination as well as your reason.

I hope to reduce your anxiety level by providing you with the tools you need to prepare and deliver as dynamic an audition as your ability and the auditioning circumstances will allow. When you understand that you have the power to exercise control over your auditions and affect the casting choice, I think you will be excited rather than overcome by the prospect of auditioning.

NOTE: *I use the term "auditors" to include the casting director, producer, director, playwright, composer, lyricist, etc., if they are present at the audition. At different times, I wear my actor's hat, my teacher's hat, or my casting director's hat. I try to make it clear when it matters.*

Auditioning

Chapter I

————

STOP SELF-SABOTAGE:

CHANGE THE ODDS!

Most people go to work in the same office, store, or factory every day; they can anticipate who will be there, what the workplace will look like, how it will feel, how their colleagues will relate to them, and how much they will be paid. With any luck, they know what is expected of them and feel confident they can fulfill their assigned tasks.

An actor's life is quite different. A large part of an actor's work is auditioning. Unlike a "regular job", there is no paycheck at the end of the week. (Wouldn't that be nice?) More important, each auditioning event is unpredictable. The script may or may not be available to you in advance. You may be given a scene to read "cold," with only a few minutes to prepare. You may have to wait five minutes or many hours. There may be hundreds of other actors waiting to audition or you may be the only one. You may be auditioning in a small office or on the stage of a large theater. You may encounter one audi- tor or twenty. The audition atmosphere may feel welcoming or hostile. You may read the scene with someone who is a trained actor, but more likely you will read the scene with someone who is not. You may never get any feedback or know why you didn't get the job.

In a worst-case scenario, what negative effect might these cir- cumstances, and the pressure of getting a job, have on you, the actor?

You don't prepare in a serious way because you are con- vinced that, since you only have a few minutes with the direc- tor, the decision will rest only on how you look, or your personal quality. (If the director thinks you're well-suited for the role, she'll direct you at the first audition, and then you'll dig in and work hard to prepare for your callback.)

You become distracted or paralyzed when confronted with your competition, and persuade yourself that everyone else is better for the role than you are.

You feel as though the entire audition is controlled by oth- ers, upon whom you are totally dependent.

You suffer a loss of confidence. You feel isolated, anxious, insecure, and negative about your talent. You know you are a better actor than you appear to be at the audition.

You are convinced that the director has already cast the role and is obliged to see you or is doing you a favor.

If the atmosphere is not overly friendly, you assume that the director has taken an instant dislike to you.

You're certain the director knows what he wants and you don't have a clue. If you make the wrong choice, you won't get the job.

Your focus is on pleasing the director, rather than on doing your work.

You believe the director is looking for a reason to reject you rather than to hire you.

The pressure to get the job either gives you too much energy, or, in an effort to deny the pressure, too little energy.

You hurry through the audition for fear of boring the director or making her fall behind schedule, so you don't take the time to experience the important moments in the script. You rush through it and virtually fly over the material rather than inhabit it.

You feel nervous; your breath is shallow; your voice becomes constricted and doesn't sound like your natural voice; your body is stiff and self-conscious.

You feel emotionally blocked, so you work technically and are unable to get in touch with your spontaneous responses.

The more important the audition, the less freedom you feel you have to "play" the scene. (When you don't care much about getting a job, you usually land it.)

You feel angry for a variety of reasons. Perhaps you didn't have much advance notice, or you've been kept waiting a long time, or your strongest competitor is in the waiting room, or the director seems hostile or unresponsive. Or you're just angry that you have to audition at all. Why don't they just offer you the job?

When you walk into the auditioning space, you feel small, fat, naked, unfocused or amateurish, or all of the above.

After the audition, you feel disappointed in yourself because you "threw away the audition." You didn't do what you feel you are capable of doing.

If you lose the job, you believe that it's because you're not as talented as the person who got it. Or you believe it's because you're not talented at all.

Does any of this sound familiar?

How can actors not feel vulnerable at auditions? It is not in the nature of actors to be thick-skinned. If actors were not sensitive human beings, how could they understand and connect and empathize with the characters they create?

So much for the worst-case scenario. By the time you finish reading this book, I hope you will know how to create a best-case scenario and stop shooting yourself in the foot.

POWER

Actors think the auditors have all the power in the auditioning process and they have none. After all, there is one part for which many actors must vie with one another; you don't decide who gets the part, the auditors do. You don't know what they are looking for; they do and won't tell you. You have to prove to them that you're talented, and overcome their hostile skepticism and disbelief that you're right for the role. Until then, you're just another actor. "Thank you. Next!" You're gone and forgotten, their victim.

The actor's misperception of the auditioning process can be crippling. Apart from disabling yourself in all of the ways suggested at the beginning of this chapter, you abdicate your own power. The more power you attribute to the auditors, the less you have. *The truth is that, without the vision and talent of the actor, the auditors are powerless, they can't do their work.* You are the key to their power. Every director has high hopes that the next actor who walks through the door—YOU—will be the one for the part. Far from eagerly anticipating the actor's abject failure, the auditors' fondest hope is that you will give a superb audition so they can cast the role and go home.

When you shed the image of yourself as victim, you can embrace the conviction that you do have the power to affect the casting choice. Your power is your individual creativity and your ability to deliver a well-prepared, lively audition that reveals your potential for playing the role. Auditors depend on the actors who audition to shape their view of the role to be cast. That's why actors get cast, not because they fit into a cookie-cutter mold the director has in mind.

Once you realize that there is a balance of power between the actor and director, you might start looking forward to the next audition.

RESISTANCE: REJECTION

Many actors resist the auditioning process without realizing it. Resistance comes in many forms. You don't find the time to pick up the script well in advance of the audition. You had a very important engagement the night before the audition and didn't start working on the script till midnight. You're certain you're not what "they" are looking for, or you decide you really don't want the job, so why invest time and energy?

Or you did make the investment. You prepared, you put yourself out there creatively and emotionally, took risks, and the auditors didn't respond. There was no feedback and you didn't get the job. You feel defeated. You don't want to put yourself into that vulnerable place again, so at the next audition you shut down. You work technically and hold back any emotional commitment. We all know where that leads, or doesn't.

The major reason actors resist preparing properly for auditions is the fear of rejection. If you don't invest yourself in the audition, then you won't be so disappointed if you don't get the job. When you don't succeed, you won't feel like a loser because, after all, you didn't really try. That is a self-protective choice. But it has serious consequences for one's career.

Rejection is a matter of perception. Even if a director auditions fifty people for one role and they all give splendid auditions, only one will get the job. Of course, it's disappointing for the others. But does it make sense for the other forty-nine to feel as though they have failed? Negativity is your enemy.

Look at athletes. The best baseball players get a hit once in every three times at bat. Tennis champions win and lose. Basketball greats have good games and bad. Their careers are developed over the long haul. The ones who are not fly-by-nights are resilient and keep working on their game. They are not stopped by a poor game or even a losing season.

By analogy, the fear of not getting cast should not stop you from doing everything you can to give a good audition. A student of mine said, "Isn't it heartbreaking to work so hard on an audition and not get it?" Maybe, but you'll get over it. And there is always the next audition. Losing because of your own lack of preparedness is a poor alternative.

Another reason for resisting the auditioning process is that you feel the level of your acting at auditions does not represent your best work. For a serious actor who has invested years in training, this is a legitimate reaction. You feel compromised because auditioning does not allow you the time or conditions to let your work evolve. You feel you will be "indicating," or showing emotional results before you are ready.

Accept as a given that you cannot do your best work at an audition. Nobody expects it of you. You are an actor who is auditioning, not an "auditioner." If you do your best work at the audition and you are hired, you will be in big trouble when you have to perform with other actors in different circumstances.

Having said that, you need not feel compromised by auditions. You can still take the high road, use your acting technique with integrity, not force results, and deliver a dynamic audition.

Actors who have a lot of experience auditioning have learned that an investment of time and energy in *every* audition pays off. Preparation will always help minimize your nervousness. Why should you "wing" the audition, find excuses to give it short shrift, feel less confident, give the director only a vague idea of your potential? Why should you continue to sabotage yourself? Don't wait to act until you get the job. If you keep resisting the auditioning process, that may never happen!

COMPETITION

Competition can be one of the most destructive elements in undermining an actor's confidence, or anyone else's. Cindy Nelson, an Olympic silver-medalist skier, advised other competitive skiers, regarding competition, "Put blinders on to focus on doing your absolute best."

Let's say you have an audition and have prepared well, made strong acting choices, and feel you are the right person for this role. You walk into the reception area and see twenty people of your age and type crowding the waiting room, all auditioning for the same role. The first time this happens, it may be a shock. Your confidence flags. You become the casting director. You decide that this one is prettier, or taller, or has a better body, that one is more talented, has more training, is more experienced, or just got a great review, etc. Many seem "righter" for the role than you. (Women are harder on themselves than men.)

Instead of focusing on your preparation for the audition, you sit in the waiting area, trying to look cool so nobody notices you busily checking out everyone else in the room. *Don't let the competition undermine you and distract you from your real work.*

Similarly, reading the Arts and Leisure section of the Sunday edition of *The New York Times* or the Calendar section of the *Los Angeles Times* when you're unemployed can be a bruising experience. "Why is he playing that role when I would have been better? Why wasn't I auditioned? That actor got the part because she just did a TV series. I should change agents. They haven't called me in weeks." It's that kind of a business. You can eat yourself alive.

Try not to make a practice of comparing your career to someone else's. In the heat of the battle, one does get angry, frustrated, jealous, competitive. However, if you take the long view, you can defuse those feelings.

Someone will always work more than you do. Someone will always have a part you wish you were playing. Someone will always have a better agent. Someone will always be getting more attention, making more money, enjoying the career you would like to have. Actors are not alone in feeling this way. In Meryle Secrest's biography, Stephen Sondheim described the usual writer's neurosis. "Everything I write is terrible, everything everybody else writes is wonderful." Don't go there! Remind yourself there is always someone else who doesn't work as much as you do, who will wish for the part you're playing, and who wants your agent, etc.

Competition is a given in our business. And it's not all bad. Competition raises professional standards. Competition should make you work harder to develop your skills so that you, too, can be a contender.

Actors should approach an audition (and indeed, their careers) with the firm belief that they have something to offer that is unique. Treasure who you are and what you bring to the audition. In Laurence Olivier's book *On Acting,* he writes, "Whatever people may have thought of my Hamlet, I think it was not bad. I know it was not perfection, but it was *mine.* I did it. It was *mine.*"

SELF-CONFIDENCE

Self-confidence is your *lifeline* in this business. If you don't believe in your talent, no one else will. I don't mean to suggest that you should be supremely overconfident and arrogant, thinking you're the only person for the job, the best there is, and patting yourself on the back. I refer to self-confidence in the deeper sense: trusting your own instincts, training, and experience to bring a role to life. If you approach each audition as though you had the job and were working on the part, you will have a much more positive mind-set going into the audition. Assume you have the ability to play the role. Casting director Jay Binder says, "For those five or ten minutes, you do have the part. No one else is in the room doing that part. It is yours. Own it."

Every person who chooses to become an actor must start out with a strong belief in his own talent. There are so many reasons not to go into this profession that to enter without that conviction makes the decision to do so reckless and whimsical. However, in the course of focusing on the job market and trying to carve out a career, you sometimes lose your feeling of excitement and optimism about acting in general and your own work in particular.

It helps to remind yourself why you wanted to become an actor in the first place. What inspired you? You may have acted in a school play, or seen a great performance, or loved to transform yourself into different characters. Perhaps a casual interest was ignited by a wonderful teacher. You experienced your own need for self-expression. Get in touch with that source. Let your imagination go back to the places, the moments, the people who inspired you in the beginning and in the course of your career.

Of course, not every actor who believes in his acting ability will necessarily succeed! But without that deep conviction, you will be in a constant and losing struggle to maintain your self-confidence. You will beat yourself up after each audition, lose heart, and undermine your ability to achieve your goal.

When you are unemployed as an actor, you tend to focus on

what's gone wrong: why you didn't get called back or didn't get the role in this or that project. You tend to forget your successes, your creative experiences, your close connection with the other members of an ensemble, the good feedback you got from a performance or an audition. I'm not suggesting you should live in the past. But I am suggesting that you perceive your career as a continuum so that the sun doesn't rise and set based on your getting one particular job.

A student of mine who is not a very good tennis player decided he would pretend he was Andre Agassi on the court and, to his delight, played better than he had ever played. If you believe you are the actor you want to be, you will feel more confident and will surely give better auditions.

THE WINDOW OF OPPORTUNITY

Auditions can only be as good as your perception of their possibilities. If you accept auditions for what they are—*an opportunity to reveal your ability to play a particular role*—auditions can be rewarding rather than punishing.

Every actor can learn to improve his or her auditioning technique. The more conscious you are of your auditioning experiences and the requirements of good auditioning, the more you will develop your skills and exercise control over the process.

Evaluate your audition. It's comforting to take the sting out of a poor audition by blaming the casting director, the script, the lack of time, the auditioning atmosphere, etc. But you should learn to differentiate between what you did and the circumstances that may have prevented you from doing good work. "Was my preparation adequate? Did I have the courage to follow my impulses? Was my work qualitatively better at home? Was I inhibited by the auditioning circumstances? Were my nerves the problem? Did I have enough energy? Was I 'pushing' my performance? Was I using myself fully? What was lacking? Was I in control? Did I make the adjustments the director asked for? If not, why not? What can I do to improve my next audition?"

Make notes of everything you learn from each audition. A less-than-perfect audition can be unsettling and prevent you from being objective immediately after the audition. If that's the case, wait to undertake this analysis until a few hours later, when you can be more objective about what happened. Your investment in post-auditioning checkups will make you aware of any particular problems you continue to have.

Apart from improving your auditioning skills, every audition can be a positive experience in a broader sense:

1. Auditions will teach you how to work quickly.

In television and film work, scripts are changed from moment to moment, and you need to incorporate those changes on the spot. In theater, new plays are frequently rewritten during previews, and changes often go into the performance the same night.

2. *Auditions will help you explore your character range.*
You may not be hired to play Hamlet or Lady Macbeth for one reason or another, but in working seriously on auditions for those roles, you may discover elements in the characters that you might not have tapped before and that you can then incorporate in other roles.

3. *Every audition has the potential for opening the door to work; if not now, then in the future.*
When you give a good audition, it will be remembered, whether or not you are cast. The auditors are in the business of finding good actors. You may get on the casting director's "Most Wanted List." You will develop a network of directors, producers, playwrights, and casting directors who will want to consider you for other projects over a long period of time. Their notion of who you are as an actor comes from an aggregate of contacts and experiences. It comes from seeing you perform, reading your reviews, hearing what other people say about you, and seeing you at auditions. (Keep a journal of every agent, casting director, director, and producer who has seen your work either in auditions or performance. Let them know about your jobs. Send them good reviews.)

4. *Auditions teach you how to direct yourself so that you can make independent choices confidently.*
There are situations apart from auditioning where this ability will be essential. If you are in a long-running play, the director

may have vanished after the first week, or may appear only occasionally to give notes. The director's assistant or the stage manager may give you notes on where your performance is losing steam or getting mechanical. But chances are he is not going to coach you on what to do about it.

If you are a replacement in a play, you are responsible for maintaining the original blocking and for interacting with the other members of the company in a way that will not require redirection. You may be "put into" the play by the stage manager. But he cannot tell you how to make your performance your own within the framework of someone else's interpretation. That is your task. Ben Brantley, critic for *The New York Times,* described successful replacements in the long-running musical *Chicago* (*The New York Times,* 7/7/99): "Replacement stars are rarely an unconditional blessing. You certainly don't want watered-down imitations of originals; on the other hand, a radical reconception of a major part can throw a production out of kilter. The satisfactions of Ms. Henshall's and Ms. d'Amboise's performances come from how they stay comfortably within an established framework while bringing their own transforming vitality."

5. Auditions provide you with a chance to act.
You have a captive audience of people who are there because they want to see your work. Good auditions can be thrilling to watch. The actor may be alone on a bare stage, or in front of a camera, script in hand. If a talented actor is fully present and

has done his homework, our imaginations will fill in the rest. If the actor is courageous and free, surprises happen that can be exciting for the actor as well as the auditors. Auditors hope for a memorable audition, not one that is predictable, ordinary, or uninspired. Go beyond the comfort zone; a good audition is not a "safe" one. George C. Scott said, "Safe actors hold back, experiment not, dare not, change nothing, and have no artistic courage. . . ."

The audition space is yours. The time is yours. Don't waste it. You may not hit it right every time, but you can certainly change the odds.

Chapter II

———■———

THE OTHER SIDE:

A DEMYSTIFICATION

Directors always want you to give your best possible audition. Even though they may not show it, they are rooting for you when you walk in the door.

One of the reasons the auditors put on a neutral face is that they have to discuss the pros and cons of all the candidates before they decide. They fear that if they are too enthusiastic, you will feel misled if you don't get the job. (Or, if you do get the job, that your agent will ask for more money!) So they may seem somewhat buttoned up.

Directors are hired to serve the script. They understand the importance of the individual actor's contribution to a successful production. They know there is no way the actor can guess precisely what the director has in mind at the audition. So they will evaluate you on *your* choices. Most directors remain flexible during auditions and avoid having a rigid or sharply defined concept of the character in advance. They hope to get insights into the character from actors who think and feel independently and with whom they sense they can collaborate.

Directors may or may not have a preconception of your character's physical appearance. Sometimes, the playwright will describe the character in physical terms, but even then, most directors will not feel bound by this description and will feel free, within the parameters of the script, to depart from it. Even if the director has a strong preconception of what the character looks like, an actor's audition can cause her to do a complete turnaround. She may end up casting an actor who bears no physical resemblance to the character as the writer or director imagined him.

In the Broadway production of Hugh Wheeler's and Stephen Sondheim's *A Little Night Music* (based on Ingmar Bergman's film *Smiles of a Summer Night*), the director, Hal Prince, had originally intended the role of Madame Armfeldt to be played by a beautiful woman in her sixties or seventies. She had spent her life having affairs with royalty who favored her with duchies, jewels, and all manner of riches. The character supplied many of the funny and touching moments in the script.

Hermione Gingold's agent at ICM, Eric Shepherd, called to tell me that his client had read the script and wanted to audition for the role. Hermione was a deliciously sardonic, witty, sophisticated actor, the right age but not remotely beautiful in any conventional sense. Nor was she usually considered for roles other than purely comedic ones. Because Hermione felt so strongly about the role, Eric asked if Hal would see her. She was determined to play the part. And he was insistent and kept calling.

Hal Prince said, "I did not want to see her and she came to the audition—made the appointment because I was in Europe. I arrived and said, 'I don't want to see her. What's she doing here?' Well, the message we got was, surely he won't refuse to give five minutes to someone who wants to audition. And I loved her the minute she came out onstage."

For her audition, Hermione chose Madame Armfeldt's last scene. Madame is sitting in her wheelchair, telling her grand-daughter a story, when suddenly her head drops forward, her wig falls off, and she dies. Unbeknownst to us, Hermione had come in wearing her own wig, and, after delivering an enchant-ing, moving performance, her head fell forward and her wig fell off. Of course, she got the job. It wasn't the wig. It was her understanding of the world of the play, her consummate skill as a performer, her love of the character, and her commitment to her acting choices. Hermione was nominated for a Tony for her performance.

When I did the American casting for *Jefferson in Paris* for James Ivory, we looked for an actor to play Jefferson's daughter, Patsy, who first appears in the film at age eleven and by the film's end is fifteen. I saw hundreds of young professionals, amateurs and nonactors, girls about thirteen or fourteen years old, and brought in a few for James. We were hoping to dis-cover a naturally gifted teenager but were not having much luck. Then Gwyneth Paltrow, who was about nineteen at the time and virtually unknown, happened to meet James and ask if she could audition for the role of Patsy. James thought she was too old for the role, but she wanted to come in anyway and he agreed, probably more as a favor than for any other reason. (We had cast her mother, Blythe Danner, in *Mr. and Mrs. Bridge*.) Gwyneth read the role with great intelligence, sensitivity, and emotional immediacy. She knocked our socks off. James decided to make the character older, because casting Gwyneth would enrich the film, even though her age would be a bit off historically. (She would start at fifteen and go to nineteen.) She gave a beautifully nuanced performance that brought the character to life in ways none of us had imagined.

I know what you're thinking. "I'm not represented by ICM and I'm not Gwyneth Paltrow." And, yes, casting directors are often resistant to pressure brought by agents who submit unknown actors who are very far afield from what the director is looking for. So, yes, it's not easy to be seen under those circumstances. However, the bottom line is: *your director may be very open to a portrayal of your character very different from what she originally had in mind.*

Directors these days are much more inclined to cast nontraditionally, to cast against type when it does not interfere with the play's concept. Women now play men's roles, actors of color play roles that were not written specifically for actors of their race or ethnicity, and age range is more flexible. (See "A Note on Nontraditional Casting" at the end of this chapter.)

Actors think the director expects them to give an opening night performance at their audition. If you make a "mistake," lose your place, or miss an important moment, all is lost! *Auditions are auditions.* It is not the director's expectation that you will hit every moment on target or give the kind of performance that evolves through a long and intense rehearsal period.

Here are the basic elements I think most directors look for at an audition:

Concentration: The most basic and important tool for an actor. You must create and maintain your own personal auditioning space, from which you exclude all else that is happening in the room, apart from you and the reader.

Feeling of Truth: You project authenticity; everything your character says and does is believable, within the style of the play.

Spontaneity: The audition "happens"; you are in touch with your impulses and feelings, and you play the scene from moment to moment.

Specificity: You are not acting "in general" or playing a "mood." You have made acting choices that are particular to the scene and the character.

Energy: What you do should never be static, passive, or casual. It should manifest creative energy, either inner, outer, or both.

Humor: You know where it is and how to play it.

Courage: You don't give a safe, neutral audition. You commit to your acting choices, without inhibition, and are willing to take risks.

Skill: You have the technique and taste needed to deliver all of the above.

I have seen Hal Prince watch an actor at an audition give a rather bland reading, in which she invested a few moments with something thoughtful, original, or dynamic. Hal would give the actor a second chance and call her back because he sensed the actor's potential. He could tell that the actor was talented, but for one reason or another was unable to spark the whole scene at his audition. Frequently, Hal was right, and the callback was often much stronger than the first audition.

Directors are not always this generous or perceptive. But some can tell the difference between a good actor having a bad day, and a bad actor giving a flash-in-the-pan audition. The latter are the first to get fired because they can't deliver in performance.

DIRECTORS ARE PEOPLE

Actors don't think of directors as ordinary human beings—people with idiosyncrasies and insecurities like themselves—or even as professional colleagues and peers.

You may be surprised to learn that some directors feel more awkward and less comfortable at auditions than the actors, particularly if the audition is in a small room (for film or television) where the actor is face-to-face with the director. Actors are more accustomed to being looked at than directors, and have a written script to follow. The director is always improvising. He may be a great director but not a good communicator, and he may find it difficult to give clear, concise adjustments to the actor on the spot.

My experiences with a few directors will give you an idea of the range of characters you might find on the other side of the table.

Woody Allen's awkwardness at auditions is legendary. As an actor, I once auditioned for one of his films. At my first meeting, I was introduced to him by his very gracious casting director Juliet Taylor. As I opened my mouth to say hello, he shook my hand and said, "Juliet told me about you. Please go outside." I had not said one word. I thought he looked me over and decided I was wrong for the role. Then, to my utter surprise, Juliet came out and gave me a scene to look at.

When I returned the next week to audition, Woody was at the opposite end of a large room—very far away. The moment I uttered the last word of the scene, he raced across the room and practically tore the script out of my hands. He said thank you and I left, rather stunned. Woody Allen is a brilliant filmmaker; some people consider him a genius. He makes films everybody wants to work in. But his eccentricities are legendary.

Even casting directors sometimes have to audition for a casting job. I was very nervous before my meeting with Bernardo

Bertolucci to discuss casting *The Last Emperor.* I remember trying to figure out what to wear. (Shall I try to look Italian, wear a
black outfit, black stockings, high heels, a raincoat?) I won-
dered whether I could ever be at ease in Bertolucci's presence.
I kept seeing images in my head from his great movie *The Con-
formist.* From the very first moment of our meeting, he made
me feel as though I were his best friend. And, within five minutes, he gave me the job. (How could you not fall in love with
such a man?)

Bertolucci is a charming, warm, gracious person who enjoys
meeting actors. Many actors who audition for him are in awe
of him, as I was. But their nervousness begins to evaporate
when they walk into the room and are met with his informal,
cheerful greeting. He listens and observes carefully, and his
directions to actors when giving adjustments are always very
specific, insightful, and provocative.

I auditioned for Jerome Robbins's production of *Mother
Courage* four times and didn't get cast. But then Jerry called
me in to audition for the original company of *Fiddler on the
Roof.* Even though I was not much of a singer, I auditioned for
the part of Hodel, who sings "Far from the Home I Love," a
song for a legitimate soprano voice. After six auditions, at
which my acting was evidently good enough but my singing
was not, Jerry had me work privately with Jerry Bock and Sheldon Harnick, the composer and the lyricist, on "Far from the
Home I Love." I sang it for the seventh audition, and clearly, I
sounded bad. I knew it. Bock and Harnick knew it. But Jerry

Robbins was determined not to give up on me. He came to my singing lesson the next week and listened to me sing all the songs I was working on. One was "Irma La Douce" which required more of a chest voice. My chest voice was not rangy, but easier to listen to than my soprano. He got very excited and said, "That's what you must sing for Bock and Harnick at the next audition!"

So I sang "Irma La Douce" at the eighth audition, and at the end of the song, Bock and Harnick stood up in the theater and one or the other (I was too spacey to tell which) called out, "She's got a chest voice! She can play Tzeitel!" I got the job. Jerry Robbins always had the reputation for being extremely difficult and demanding. But, in this case, his persistence and determination on my behalf were awesome. (Nowadays, after the fifth audition you get paid.)

I sat with Hal Prince at auditions for fourteen years. Actors always felt his support and enthusiasm for their efforts. Hal has a great respect for talent, almost a sense of wonder. I remember at Teri Ralston's audition for the role of Jenny in *Company,* he turned to Steve Sondheim and George Furth and me, and said, "That's the most beautiful voice I ever heard!" And then he repeated his praise to her. (She was, indeed, cast.) It was impossible for Hal to be neutral when he really loved an actor's work.

These were the days when we auditioned in Broadway the-aters (not done much anymore). Hal would get a glimmer of something an actor did that provoked him in some way. He would run down the aisle, hop on stage, give a direction, and run back. Hal didn't care if the actors had an extensive résumé. He was interested only in what the actor could deliver, so we gave lots of performers their first Broadway jobs. Hal has great casting instincts; he knew the difference between dazzle and authenticity, and always recognized the real thing. In my fourteen years as his casting director, he only fired one performer from any of his shows. The reason was that she couldn't sing a song that had been written for her character after she was cast. He felt terrible about it.

Some young, inexperienced directors are awkward at auditions. They may not know how to evaluate actors and are trying to act as though they do. What the actor sometimes sees is insecurity masked in overly authoritative behavior. They're playing the role of "Director" without the background that allows them to feel at ease in the role.

There are other young directors who are insightful and smart. Brad Silberling had an idea of the character I auditioned for in the film *City of Angels* that was not on the page and that I certainly did not deliver in my audition. I did not have the whole script, the audition scene was short, but I did my best to bring a feeling of truth to what I imagined was the situation in the scene. After I read, he told me the prior circumstances and gave me an adjustment quite different to what I had done originally. I left feeling I had overplayed the adjustment and messed up the audition. I was totally surprised when I found out I was cast. Brad evidently saw my potential for playing the role, in spite of what I thought was not a good audition. Many directors need to see exactly what you will be doing for a film, since there is usually no rehearsal, but Brad was a confident young director who gave me the benefit of the doubt.

Actors always like to audition for directors who are or once were actors. The adjustments they give to actors are more process-oriented than ones given by directors who have never studied acting. Elia Kazan, Jerry Zaks, Michael Mayer, and Scott Ellis are all theater directors who were actors before they became directors. Kazan frequently worked with actors at auditions as though they were cast and at a rehearsal. I have had experience casting for both Jerry Zaks and Scott Ellis, who work extensively at auditions with actors who interest them. This encourages and often relaxes the actor, and tells the director a lot about the actor's potential and whether she can take direction and should be called back or cast. Scott has his own method for evaluating auditions. After each audition, he classifies the actor as follows:

1. Shouldn't be in the business
2. Good actor
3. Possible for the role
4. That's it—got the job

Some directors, of course, play the power game. Some are abusive. I remember an audition I had with a major L.A. television producer who was auditioning me for a pilot. I walked into the room, where he was sitting behind a table, reading. The casting director announced my name, and he kept on reading. I did the audition, and when I finished and looked up, he was still reading. The casting director said, "Thank you, Joanna," and I walked out. The director never said a word. Woody Allen looked like Prince Charming after this guy. Another woman who had gone in before me was still out in the reception area. He had behaved the same way to her. We were both furious and humiliated, railing at his craziness. We complained to the casting director, who was beside herself at the way the actors were treated, and apologized profusely.

The odd thing was that I was called back. I didn't want to go through an audition with this director again, but my agent thought I shouldn't pass it up because it was a good project. The director behaved very differently. He was not reading this time, actually said hello, thank you, and goodbye. Perhaps the casting director had spoken to him. Go figure.

On the subject of directors, Nora Ephron, screen writer and director, says, "I started going to auditions when we did *Silkwood*, so I watched Mike Nichols audition actors, one after another. Mike is the kindest, most generous of auditioners—he always takes a huge amount of time talking to the actor before they have to read, and he's charming and would put anyone at ease. Except, of course, for an actor who is auditioning for one of his movies. I cannot tell you how many of them *started smoking again* during one of his charming and relaxing chats. The point being that I learned, immediately, that auditioning is as painful and difficult a thing as anyone ever goes through, and I've tried to at least do a pale imitation of Mike when I audition actors.

Just last year I heard about a fellow director who recently had her hair blown out while auditioning an actor. And I have worked with directors who don't even like to meet actors—who do everything on videotape. Which is also unimaginable to me. I find it much easier to judge performance when I'm in the room than when I look at a tape."

Most of the directors you will audition for are friendly, pleasant, and professional. However, you need to be prepared for anything and everyone. Crazies included.

INTERVIEWS

I was cast in *The Killing Fields* solely on the basis of an interview with the director, Roland Joffé. At the time, my older daughter had just gone off to college and I was feeling bereft. In spite of my serious interest in what *The Killing Fields* was about, my attention was not so much on getting the role as it was on the absence of my daughter. Because of the warm and friendly atmosphere that Joffé brought to the interview, and the somewhat distracted state I was in, I mentioned my feelings to him. He was very interested in what I had to say about my relationship with my daughter, and took a generous amount of time to listen and respond. It was only in retrospect that I realized Joffé had probably seen in me that afternoon the qualities he was looking for in the character. The character was also a mother, and had a close and compassionate relationship with her brother.

If I had been up for a role in a sitcom that day, I would have had to try to think of something to make me feel better so I could appear light, easy, and funny. When we perform, we usually have to enter a different atmosphere from the one we happen to be in at the time. Interviews and auditions are no different.

Interviewers are interested in getting a sense of who you are, apart from what you've done. (They usually have your résumé in front of them.) *Interviews are conversations that invite you to be yourself.* Don't be too businesslike or negate what's interesting about yourself. Try not to answer questions with just a yes or no. Have something to talk about that enlivens and engages you, something that you feel passionate about. (It could be, "I started to act because I saw blah give a great performance in blah. . . . Did you see it? She did such and such that was so surprising and funny." Or, "This script reminds me of a true story I read about. . . ." Or even, "A funny thing happened to me on the way here. . . .") Whatever you decide to talk about should not be "scripted"! You want to improvise in the moment, be spontaneous and interesting.

Some directors and casting directors are not good interviewers. They hope you will share the burden of coming up with questions and topics for discussion. You can ask them questions about themselves. "How did you go from acting to direct-ing?" It helps to have some information about them so you can ask informed questions.

James Lapine speaks about a hypothetical meeting with an actor who is under consideration for a large role in a film and who has had the opportunity to read the script. Says Lapine, "The actor should have an opinion on what he would do with the role. If he only meets with the director and doesn't audi-tion, it may be more difficult for the director to go against type unless the actor can talk about how he sees the character. I like the sucker job—'Gee, it's an interesting script,' rather than being critical. We're all so insecure."

AUDITIONING ATMOSPHERE

Jenny, the four-year-old daughter of a friend of mine, asked at breakfast one day, "Mommy, would you get undressed in front of a dog?" Jenny was questioning adult inhibitions. Inhibitions are one of the actor's worst enemies. You must be able to act for any and all auditors, dogs and all, and not be dependent on their responses or on finding a friendly atmosphere at the audi-tion.

It can be intimidating to walk into a space where a stranger or a group of strangers is waiting to evaluate your work. If you walk into the audition room and feel what you interpret as a cold, unfriendly atmosphere, and no one is smiling or talking to you, you tend to think negative thoughts. "They hate the way I look. They didn't know I had red hair. They think I'm too young, too short, too thin, or not ethnic enough. They're wondering why the casting director called me in. They realize now it was a mistake. How can I expose myself emotionally when they seem so hostile?"

A student of mine had an audition scene that was full of sexual language. She walked into the audition room, took one look at the group of five men behind the table, and her courage failed her. She could not play the scene the way she had prepared it. She left feeling that she had virtually thrown away her audition. *Know what your inhibitions are and have the courage to transcend them.* Otherwise, you will sabotage your audition and will be unable to reveal your ability to play a role. (I'm not suggesting you take off your clothes!)

The hardest audition to do in an unwelcoming atmosphere is comedy. You have found the humor in the scene and are feeling great about your acting choices. As a matter of fact, every time you rehearsed it, you had a hard time keeping yourself from laughing. You start the scene and it is as though the auditors are not hearing you or are asleep. You freak out. The reality may be that they have heard that scene so many times they can't manage to laugh out loud no matter who is reading it. After your audition, they all agree that you're the new Jackie Mason, Jim Carrey, Sandra Bernhard, Mike Meyers, Dame Edna, or whomever, and hire you. But they may not even snicker at the audition. Ride it through as though they're falling off their chairs laughing. You never know.

Actors fantasize about walking into an auditioning space and finding the auditors acting like hosts at a party: welcoming, friendly, and warm, greeting you like a long lost friend. If the auditors are relaxed, drinking coffee, and engage you in conversation, you might think to yourself, "We're having a nice conversation. They seem to be interested in me. I feel very comfortable. I might get this part. I'm not nervous anymore. This is great." Then you start the audition and your work goes right out the window. You have lost your "performance consciousness." If you have prepared properly and come in ready to work, and the audition seems like a party, enjoy it, but be aware of what you need to do to get back on track. Before you start your audition, you will need to take a few moments to connect with what I call your "pre-beat" (see Chapter III) before you begin your audition.

Often, you have been called in by the casting director and you have never met the director. Therefore, when the director sees you for the first time as you walk into the audition room, you look for a hopeful sign that she is, indeed, pleased with your "look" and interested in you for the role. Your heart may sink if the director does not seem particularly friendly. You may perceive her to be disinterested, which is probably not the case. (It's that neutral mask; if she were interested or disinterested, she probably wouldn't show it.)

If the director is a friend or someone you have worked with on another project, you feel certain she will respond warmly when you enter the room, so you are disappointed when it doesn't happen. Understand the director's dilemma: as a professional, she is trying to maintain her neutrality. And if ultimately she decides to cast you, she doesn't want anyone to think she was showing favoritism or was influenced by her relationship with you.

Sometimes the auditors will whisper to each other during your audition. This can be terribly distracting. You decide they are totally bored, hate you and your audition, and are talking about what to order for lunch. But, in truth, they may talk to each other during your audition because they are interested in you. (They probably wouldn't bother to confer if they were totally turned off.) They may be trying to decide if you will be a good match with another actor they've cast, or whether they want to have you stay and look at another scene, or another role, or whether to redirect you, etc. They often need to make these decisions while you are in front of them. Keep your focus, do your work, and don't be distracted by what's happening on the auditors' side of the room.

I believe most casting directors, directors, et al. try to conduct the business of auditioning with grace. But, if you can believe it, they often feel more pressured than you do. You have one audition. They may see fifty or more actors that day. They don't want to pass over anyone who might be a good possibility. They have only a few minutes to evaluate each actor's talent and appropriateness for the role. They're already an hour behind schedule and the director has to get to the airport. The actor who is cast will be their choice, so their professional reputation is, in some measure, on the line. It is a commonly held belief that casting is the largest single factor (some say 90 percent) in the success or failure of a project. And directors have a lot on their plate besides casting. They are responsible for the overall look of the show or film (sets, lighting, costumes, props), the budget, and the production schedule. All of these elements are cooking in the preproduction period, when the show is cast. That's a lot of pressure.

There are casting deadlines. There is often lots of money involved. There may be disagreement among the producers, director, playwright, casting director about how to cast a particular role. That might make them nervous and edgy. A wag described auditions as a bunch of nervous people being judged by a bunch of nervous people.

Most auditors will be sensitive to the pressures of the auditioning event for the actor and will try to create a comfortable auditioning atmosphere. But don't be surprised if there is something else in the air. If there is, chances are it's not you. They're just not good enough actors to disguise whatever may have happened in the room before you came in. (Are you beginning to feel happier being on your side of the table?)

If there is a way to use any of your feelings that bubble up in the auditioning room atmosphere, whatever they may be, try to integrate them. They'll be filled with life! In any event, don't let the auditioning room atmosphere rock you or rob you of your power to do your personal best. *Create your own acting space, a space that is not dependent on the atmosphere in the room.*

TALENT IS NOT ALL

Casting a show is a little like making sausage: you don't really want to know what goes into it. But, just so you don't beat up on yourself if you've done your best and still not landed the job, here are a few of the possible reasons you may not get hired:

The director doesn't have any conception of what she's looking for. She is simply unable to make a decision until she has seen everyone in the U.S. By that time, she may have forgotten the good people she saw at the beginning of the auditioning process and doesn't heed the casting director's pleas on whom to call back. (Fortunately, for film and television they can use videotape.)

The director has a powerful preconception of the character. It requires a particular physical type which you're not.

The family relationships among the cast of characters make age, size, and coloring important to the director in casting your role. You don't fit.

The look of the show; you're not it and she is not enlightened about nontraditional casting.

You may be too similar to another actor already cast and the director is looking for a contrasting type.

You may be too tall, too short, or otherwise not a good match to play opposite the star.

All you've done is theater. The network or the studio doesn't want to take a chance on you for the leading role in a movie or TV show.

You are too well-known as the star of a popular TV series, and they're looking for unknowns.

You're on the callback list but time has run out. They can only call back a portion of the actors on the list. They make an arbitrary decision to call back a few names on the list and you are not included.

You audition to replace an actor in a theatrical production. The costumes cost a fortune. The producers won't consider any-one who can't fit into the departing actor's clothes.

You don't have enough of a box-office name or enough profes-sional experience for a starring role.

The director may have an irrational subjective response to your looks, your speech, whatever. You remind him of someone he doesn't want to be in the room with every day.

The director got out on the wrong side of the you-know-what that morning.

Casting is sometimes done by committee. The producer has a favorite. The director has another favorite. They can only agree on someone who isn't anybody's favorite but is acceptable to all concerned. That person gets the role. You were one of the favorites. What a bummer. You gave a great audition. He'll cast you next time.

Most directors take their job seriously and make the effort to pick the most talented actor who is best suited for the role. But sometimes they make a mistake; it's the human condition.

A NOTE ON
NONTRADITIONAL CASTING

Nontraditional casting refers to the casting of actors of color, a female actor, or an actor with disabilities in a role where race, ethnicity, gender, or physical capability is not essential to the character's or play's development.

Where Are We?

The movement for inclusion in casting has raised the consciousness of the performing arts community. Many agents, casting directors, directors, playwrights, and producers are now proactive on this issue. Although there is still a long way to go to achieve casting that recognizes talent over color, gender, or disability, measurable progress has been made.

If you are an actor of color or disability, broaden your vision. Go to every casting call for a character you might play. Include in your repertoire of monologues characters you do well, whether or not the roles are specific to your race, ethnicity, gender, or disability. Talk to your agent about your desire and capacity to be submitted for diverse roles. Agents need to be assertive on behalf of clients whom they believe to be talented and capable of playing many different roles.

The Non-Traditional Casting Project in New York City has created a file of pictures and résumés of actors of color and disability from all over the United States. Be sure to send in your picture and résumé; if you are already in the file, update your information regularly. There is no cost to you or to the casting directors who use it extensively.

All the performers' unions have offices that promote employment opportunities for actors of color and disability. Screen Actors Guild has an affirmative-action file and department. Both Actors' Equity Association and the American Federation of Television and Radio Artists have offices of equal employment opportunity and there is a triunion file of performers with disabilities.

Chapter III

———————————

ACTABLE CHOICES

What is an actable choice? It is a choice, rooted in the text, that incites you to act, a choice that marshals your intuition, imagination, senses, and reason to help bring the text and the character to life.

An unactable choice may be based on a correct idea or a reasonable interpretation of the text, but it is acting from the neck up; talking—yada, yada, yada—based on a rational analysis and knowledge of the text. It might get you an "A" in a college essay but it won't get you the part. *For your audition, you must translate ideas into actable choices.*

The ten questions posed in this chapter are designed to help you *mine* the scene and the character. They are meant to set you on a path that will stimulate your imagination as well as your mind. The actable choices support and reinforce each other, encourage you to flesh out the material, and discourage you from rushing into a cliché performance at an audition.

Because acting is such a competitive profession and auditions hard to come by, actors sometimes flail about, searching for acting choices that are wildly different. They hope to show off their special talent, whether or not the choice has anything to do with the audition material. They look for original interpretations to shock or surprise the director. They hope their "originality" will be memorable. The actor's secret fantasy is that if he is sufficiently unpredictable, different, or interesting, the director will leap up from his chair and shout, "I've never seen anything like this before! You've got the job!"

Not quite. You must connect with what the playwright wrote. You can be surprising, inventive, and unpredictable, and still be rooted in the text. The playwright or director has not charged the actor with the task of reinterpreting the text. An audition that is surprising and offbeat but has little to do with the material at hand is ultimately self-defeating. Focus on what is knowable about the text, not what is unknowable; otherwise, the auditors won't be able to evaluate your performance. Play the play!

Actors looking for motivations sometimes invent backgrounds or relationships that are not even implied in the scene. In my auditioning workshop, a student was doing a scene from the film *Fame*, in which a voyeur, who is posing as a filmmaker, has invited a young woman to his apartment to get her to take off blouse in front of a video camera. It is a simple scenario, but the student was not playing the action of the scene. When I asked him what he was doing, he said he had decided that the young woman was his ex-girlfriend's sister, and he was getting revenge on his girlfriend for dumping him. His reading made no sense because of what he was imposing on the scene. Respect the text!

When you practice applying the ten actable choice questions, you will begin to develop a sixth sense for the *clues* in the text that will help you focus on information that leads you to action. Having prepared in this way, you will feel grounded in the text and can then trust your creative impulses at the audition, allowing you to play the scene freely and spontaneously.

The vocabulary used in this chapter should be understandable to anyone who has studied acting. It describes tools that can be easily incorporated into any auditioning technique. My goal is to help you find the life in the scene and deliver it at the audition.

Here are ten questions that will lead you to actable choices:

1. What are your first impressions, your immediate intuitive responses to the scene?
2. What is the world of the play?
3. What is the scene about?
4. Who is the character?
5. What is the character's objective?
6. What is the obstacle to achieving the objective?

7. What are the relationships in the scene?

8. Where are the "moments" in the scene?

9. What is the atmosphere of the scene?

10. What is the pre-beat?

Let us consider the questions one by one.

1. What are your first impressions, your immediate intuitive responses to the scene?

Treasure your first impressions. Honor your intuition. If the auditioning circumstances allow you the time, find a quiet place to read the material where you won't be disturbed. Become an innocent, open yourself to your imagination. *Your first impressions are a reliable guide, a direct response to the human behavior in the scene.*

Even when time is short, don't skim the scene the first time through. Read the scene (or, better still, the entire play or script, if it is available) for a "feeling of the whole," as Michael Chekhov describes it. Often there is a tendency to focus only on the character for which you are auditioning, and all other information is perilously ignored.

What are the images, feelings, and ideas the play arouses in you? Are the scene, the character, or the relationships evocative of anything in your own experience or imagination? If you "listen" to the text with your imagination as well as your mind, you will let the style, atmosphere, and energy of the scene into your consciousness. You will see the characters move and hear them speak. You will sense their visceral needs. *Don't hurry into analysis*. The freer your imagination, the more the scene will come into focus.

If you censor or disregard your intuitive responses out of a lack of trust in yourself or out of inhibition, the true meaning of the scene will elude you. Actors often feel the words and ideas in the text are all they have to hold onto at an audition. However, in doing so, they reduce rather than enhance the life of the text, which is the actor's job. Mining a script should be a little like reading tea leaves. You should search for meaning in the slightest, most subtle shifts of thought, feeling, or desire.

Stanley Kubrick was quoted as saying, "The hardest thing in making a movie is to keep in the front of your consciousness your original response to the material. Because that's going to be the thing that will make the movie." The same applies to auditioning.

Your first impressions are not what you present at the audition. But they will inform your presentation and resonate in your audition performance. I find it interesting to think back on my initial impressions upon reading a play in which I later appeared. The performance went through many different phases in the rehearsal process, but I can always trace some of the elements in the final performance to my initial responses to the material.

After seeing *Murder in the First*, a film starring Kevin Bacon about a prisoner who had been in solitary confinement for three years, I asked Kevin how he arrived at his performance, which required a radical transformation. He said, "When I read the script the first time, I heard the character's voice."

For an actor, there is nothing quite so exciting as starting to read a script for the first time. (Never mind that we are often disappointed in the material because it is poorly written!) When I am handed a script for an audition, I take it home with me like an unopened box of chocolates (I'm wearing my actor's hat now). I want desperately to open the box and sample a few. The temptation to read the script on the elevator, the subway, the cashier's line at the supermarket, is overpowering. To wait until I get home is the worst kind of punishment. However, if I manage to wait till I get to a quiet place and fully use my actor's concentration on the first few readings, I know I am more likely to get in touch with the underlying meaning of the text. My early impressions and intuitive responses will be more accessible and more true.

Read the auditioning scene silently a few times before speaking the lines. If you wait to speak aloud, your line readings are more likely to unite the words with the subtext. The subtext will then bubble up to the surface. Actors usually feel the need to speak the lines instantly, so holding back takes some willpower. I promise you, the rewards will be worth the effort. Federico Fellini observed, "If there were a little more silence, if we all kept quiet . . . maybe we could understand something!"

You have a powerful imagination that is ready to serve you,

to inspire you, but you need to provide it with the right atmosphere. It doesn't much like crowded buses.

2. *What is the world of the play?*

Enter the world of each play. I'm not suggesting you write a doctoral dissertation on the play. However, *your acting choices should be determined, in part, by the visual and sensory images of the period and place represented, and the unique quality and tone of the piece.* How does the time and place affect the character's physical life, speech, manner, point of view? What is the social class of the character? What does the furniture look like? How does the clothing feel? Is it loose or constricting? What is its texture? (Silk and velvet feel very different than rough muslin or wool.) Smelling the dust and dirt in *The Grapes of Wrath* or the perfumed wigs in *A School for Scandal* will quickly immerse you in the world of the play. Even the music of the period—waltz, minuet, jazz, swing, pop, or rap—may suggest the world of the play.

Sir John Gielgud said of Beverley Cross in the part of Balthazar in *Much Ado About Nothing*, "You'll never make an actor. You wear your doublet and hose like a blazer and flannels." You won't wear a costume for your auditions. But your posture and physical behavior must look and feel as though you are fully costumed.

The physical and vocal elements in your work must be organically rooted in the character's behavior in the specific circumstances of the scene. Juliet *must* speak in iambic pentameter; otherwise, she could not express her yearning for Romeo so passionately. The characters in David Mamet's *Glengarry Glen Ross must* speak and behave as they do; otherwise they couldn't con their customers and each other so convincingly. Develop your skills and techniques so that you can make these necessary adjustments quickly. Kevin Costner got away with playing Robin Hood as a contemporary American, but if you auditioned with Costner's accent and manner, you would never have been cast!

If your choices at the preliminary audition are not informed by a keen sense of the period, place, and physical elements of the scene, the director may have little time in the rush of the auditioning process to give you a second chance, even if your audition is otherwise interesting to him. *A Little Night Music* is set in Sweden in the 1900s. The world of the play is mannered and elegant. The director, Hal Prince, frequently eliminated talented actor-singers because they were "too contemporary." A minor adjustment at the audition might have been enough to establish the actor's ability to be believable in the world of the play.

At an audition, where you are often sitting or standing in one place with one arm holding the script, you need do very little to suggest the world of the play. But if you ignore it, you'll blow the audition. The director needs to know if you can create authenticity in your performance.

If you haven't read the whole script, it may be unclear to you whether the play is a comedy or drama. Don't be afraid to ask the casting director, or whomever you can ask, in advance of the audition. It serves the casting director to help you, as the answer will enable you to give a better reading.

3. *What is the scene about?*

Acting choices flow from the story or event around which the scene revolves. Try to describe the story simply, eliminating the details. *At this point, you are not concerned with how or why the event happens, only with what happens in the scene.*

What are the "given circumstances" of the auditioning scene? Given circumstances are events that happen before the scene begins that help define what happens in the scene. If you have not read the whole script, but only the auditioning scene, you may be able to figure out what came before by the information contained in the scene. If the scene is inscrutable, ask the casting director for this information before the audition, in time to integrate it into the scene. If that is impossible, you can ask the director or casting director just before you begin the audition. (But beware: new information may rob you of your preparation. Balance the benefits of getting new information and having to integrate it on the spot with going ahead with your choices based on intuition and common sense.)

In shooting a film, a "one-line schedule" is issued, in which the script is broken down scene-by-scene, describing each scene as a means of identifying it for the cast and crew. (Scenes in a film are usually very short, so they can be described easily in one sentence.) "One-liners" are the barest bones of the scene, but they give you an idea of what the scene is about. Here are a few excerpts from the "One-liner" for the Merchant-Ivory film *Mr. and Mrs. Bridge*.

> Mrs. Bridge tells Mr. Bridge that he only thinks of himself.
> Mr. Bridge questions Douglas about the gun.
> Alice realizes her visit was a mistake.
> Mr. Bridge forbids the engagement.
> The pineapple bread is a flop.
> Mrs. Bridge tells Mr. Bridge that Grace has passed away.
> Mr. Bridge finds a nude magazine in Douglas's room.

Scenes from plays are usually longer and more complicated than scenes for film and television, so what happens may be more complicated, but the idea is the same.

Think of your audition scene as a one-act play. Finding the beginning, middle, and end will help to clarify the story. The development of the story is found through new information, changes in objective, transitions, etc. that move the scene forward. You will find it helpful to identify "what happens" by naming the beginning, middle, and end with a word or phrase or a line from the script that characterizes the section.

The end of the scene should be inherent in the beginning. Look for ways that you can plant the seeds of the end in the first beat of the scene. This does not mean *playing* the end of the scene in the first beat! You are preparing the way for the end of the scene so that it doesn't come out of the blue. Look for the contrast between the beginning and end. The contrast might be subtle but important to note. The more contrast, the more dynamic the journey you chart for yourself. Film and television scenes are often fragments, so it is difficult to think of the scene as a complete entity. However, every scene is always about something, and develops in some way from beginning to end.

Asking the question "What is the scene about?" will protect you from imposing choices arbitrarily. If you don't know what happens in the scene, you will be unable to make choices that are grounded in the text and relate to the story. *Don't miss the big picture!* It will provide you with a structure for your actable choices.

4. Who is the character?

Do you really want to play the same old tune at every audition? (Jules Feiffer calls this an "as is" actor.) You have hundreds of colors and qualities within you. Some are reflected in your everyday behavior, others are rarely called upon. But they are all available to you. The teacher and director Joseph Anthony said, in discussing character, "A violin can be a trumpet."

Directors don't expect you to come to an audition with a fully defined and detailed characterization. However, there are simple and immediate ways to *evoke* a character that will show you have the potential to transform yourself.

Michael Chekhov urges the actor to explore the main *simi-*

larities and differences between himself and the character. I think his suggestion works very well for auditions. It is a quick and definitive approach to each character's particular qualities.

First, try to find yourself in the character. The similar qualities you share will seem natural and familiar, and can be easily incorporated into the part. Personal connections will resonate in an authentic way. They may need to be reduced or exaggerated. For instance, if humor is a major element in the character, and you, too, are funny or clever, you may have to make an adjustment if the character is more clownish than you are. If humor is not one of your natural gifts, then the clownishness will serve as a difference that can evoke the character. Using such differences to evoke a character is not only possible, but part of the fun of acting.

When I auditioned for the film *Class Action,* I identified very strongly with my character; her intellect, interests, and emotions seemed much like my own. But she was more assertive and confrontational than I am. Once I was aware of that difference, I tried to incorporate it into my audition. When we were shooting the film, the director, Michael Apted, indicated that I needed to make my character even stronger. Evidently, what I had shown at the audition was sufficient to suggest I could deliver that aspect of the character. You don't have to do it all at the audition. But reveal enough to let the director glean what you're capable of doing.

An immediate way to evoke the physical life of the character is to imagine the way the character might walk. Observe people on the street and you instantly get a sense of who they are by their walk; their lightness or heaviness, their pace, their grace or awkwardness, their stride, tells you a great deal about them. Imagine your character walking down the street. When you're rehearsing at home, put on shoes that the character might wear, and walk around performing your daily activities. You might wear those shoes to your audition. Even if you don't move at all during the audition, your connection to the character will be in your body.

(I was working with a student who was doing one of Portia's monologues from *Julius Caesar.* She was wearing heavy shoes with very clunky heels, the sort that were popular in the late 1990s. There was no way she could have felt or projected Portia's grace or femininity in those shoes! A more delicate shoe with a small heel made a real difference.)

Finding polarities in the character—qualities opposite from the character's principal qualities—may help you give more dimension to your audition. Tough gangsters can be sentimental, caring mothers can be fierce, heroes can have weaknesses. None of us are always in one mode, nor are fictional characters. If they appear to be, they frequently seem like clichés, predictable and dull. If you are sensitive to the specificity of the text, you can usually find moments of polarity.

To sum up, evoking a character can be simple and immediate:

1. Find the similarities and the differences.
2. Find the way the character walks.
3. Find the polarities.

5. What is the character's objective?

Henriette d'Angeville climbed to the top of Mont Blanc in 1838, where she carved a motto into the ice: "Vouloir, c'est pouvoir." ("Will is power.") Deepak Chopra puts it somewhat differently: "Desire animates us." Desire and the will to achieve what we want is the fire in our belly, our most powerful energy source. They illuminate the logic of our behavior.

What is your character's objective or aim? *What does he or she want to do in the scene?* A character cannot exist on the stage without wanting something. That want, which we will refer to as an objective, will give you a clarity of purpose and awaken your will. It is frequently the driving force in the scene. (In your training, you may have used the word "intention" instead of "objective," but the words mean the same thing.)

What the character says and does in the scene will reflect his objective in some way, even if the character is not conscious of his own objective. Often, in life, we act on needs of which we are not consciously aware. If the character *is* conscious of his objective, it is often his secret. However, *the actor must always know the character's objective even if the character is not aware of it.* For example, in Arthur Miller's *View from the*

Bridge, Eddie Carbone is in love with his niece, but has buried or repressed his feelings. His objective might be to embrace her or kiss her, but he cannot admit that desire to himself. The actor can use that objective in a powerful way to shape Eddie's behavior in the play.

Verbs define objectives. Many verbs embrace the same objective. But some verbs are more active, will turn you on, raise the stakes, e.g., dazzle instead of impress, seize instead of take. The higher the stakes, the more juice will be pumped into your work. *You can then decide how much or how little of the character's desire you want to reveal when you are auditioning for the part.*

Here are some examples of ways you can translate lackluster verbs to more dynamic ones:

Negative objectives can be turned into positive objectives. For example, "I don't want to listen" can become "I want to shut you out." "I don't want to stay here" can become "I want to get out of here."

Static "to be" verbs can be similarly transformed into more energized, active ones. "I want to be happy" can become "I want to cheer up." "I want to be funny" can become "I want to make you laugh" or "I want to play." "I want to be beautiful" can become "I want to attract you."

Watch out for casual objectives: "I want to think about it," "I want to sit here," "I want to hold on," etc. They won't give you the impulse for action.

The initial objective that launches you into the scene should be strong enough to charge you up. You can then concentrate on moment-to-moment work, which will be grounded by the objective.

An objective can change in the course of the scene. If you achieve it, you need to replace it with a different objective.

Sometimes the script lacks clarity, or you don't have time to wrap words around your character's objective. In those instances, try to be aware of your sensory or visceral responses to what the character wants to do. In this way, even without verbalizing the character's objectives, they can still serve as actable choices.

ACTIONS

Once you light the fire in your belly, you need to find ways to fight for your objective. These are your actions. They supply you with the way you achieve your objective—the "how." If your objective is to punish me, your actions may be to belittle me, to insult me, to intimidate me. Identify your actions so that you have something to play throughout the whole scene; otherwise you may lose energy in the middle.

Often, objectives and actions are verbalized in the script. "I'd like to kill that guy!" Your character doesn't necessarily mean he intends to murder someone; he may be using a figure of speech to describe his anger or irritation at a guy who was late delivering pizzas to a party. Nonetheless, "to kill" might be your action while waiting for the pizza delivery, it pumps up the character's desire to consume the pizza.

While watching actors perform in theatre or film, try to discern what their objectives and actions seem to be, or perhaps, what they should have been to create a more focused and dynamic performance.

PSYCHOLOGICAL GESTURE

Many active verbs project an image of a movement or gesture. If such a gesture is projected by your defined objective or action, try to make the gesture physically, at home, in the largest way possible, to bring the objective into your body. Find a sound or word that arises from the gesture. After making the gesture several times, try saying some of the lines while making the gesture. Then imagine yourself making it inwardly without moving. The gesture will resonate in your work as an impulse for whatever your objective or action may be. It will help you connect body and mind. (For more information on psychological gesture, see Michael Chekhov's *On the Technique of Acting*.)

Words are subjective; you will respond more to some than to others. The following is a list of active verbs that usually trigger a visceral response. Add your own verbs to the list as you discover them. A caveat: Don't pick a verb arbitrarily as though you were picking food from a menu. The verb must describe your character's objective, as it applies to your scene, in a specific way; otherwise it will mislead you and send you in the wrong direction.

List of Objectives and Actions

annihilate	corrupt	heal
awaken	dazzle	humiliate
arouse	demean	illuminate
badger	devour	incite
bait	discover	inflame
balance	dissect	inspire
bang	distract	intimidate
beat	dominate	jolt
beguile	elevate	kick
bend	embrace	kiss
blitz	eviscerate	lift
bombard	exalt	manipulate
bury	expose	mask
charm	fascinate	mold
choke	feed	nail
close	fill	nurture
command	flatten	offer
conquer	fly	oil
console	force	open
consume	grab	overwhelm
control	grasp	penetrate

pinch	scare	strengthen
please	screw	strip
poison	seduce	suck
poke	seize	tantalize
possess	serve	taste
probe	shake	tear
protect	shed	tempt
provoke	shine	threaten
pull	shock	trick
purge	slap	transcend
push	smooth	trap
quench	soar	twist
reveal	soil	uncover
rip	soothe	unite
root out	stalk	uplift
rule	stop	wring

6. *What is the obstacle to achieving the objective?*

Your objective, once defined, leads you to strong actable choices as you fight for it against an obstacle or obstacles: someone or something, external or internal, that stands between you and what you want. If there are no obstacles in your path, there will be no conflict. Without conflict, the audience will go to sleep.

Uta Hagen provides a simple illustration of objective and obstacle. There is a fire in the room and you want to get out.

The door is stuck. The harder you try to open the door, the more frustrated you become and the harder you pry and push and knock and bang. Without the obstacle, you would open the door and leave, along with the drama.

If my character is at a fancy dinner party and has not eaten for two days, her objective might be to stuff down the food very quickly. Her obstacle is her desire to appear socially acceptable.

If Hamlet's objective is to revenge his father's death, his obstacle comes from within himself: his lack of resolve, his melancholia, his fear of dying, or his madness (depending on which interpretation we're talking about and at what point in the play).

It's helpful to say to yourself, "I want to do this, but . . ." The "but" is your obstacle. The character's own feelings of anger, bitterness, excitement, urgency, etc. are sometimes obstacles that you must fight or repress in order to achieve your objective.

The scene I mentioned earlier from *Fame* starts with the young woman's entrance into the apartment of a filmmaker/voyeur. The voyeur pretends to be an auteur; he flatters her, he reassures her, he says that she should be in films, and, finally, he requests that she sit down in front of the camera and take off her blouse.

His objective might be to devour her image on film. We can assume he is feeling sexy in anticipation from the moment she walks in the door. If she senses he is "hot," she might run away before he gets her to undress. Using his sexual excitement as an obstacle makes the scene dangerous and alive. He is fighting to hide a powerful physical state of being. Physical conditions as obstacles to your objective often inspire an immediate response that strengthens your objective. These obstacles need not be externalized, but they will give you something internally to play against in fighting to achieve your objective.

Judi Dench, who is quite small physically (though towering in her talent), was cast as Lady Macbeth. She was asked how she felt when Coral Browne said, "Judi Dench playing Lady Macbeth? Her letter scene will become a postcard scene." Ms. Dench's response after howling loudly was, "I like that best. You know, something to get over."

7. *What are the relationships in the scene?*

What is the relationship between your character and the other characters, present or referred to, in the scene? The relationships between the characters will always inform and deepen the scene in some way. They may define your character. Biff can be defined by his relationship with his father, Willy Loman, in *Death of a Salesman*; Gertrude in *Hamlet* by her relationship with Claudius; Nora in *A Doll's House* by her relationship with Torvald.

Actors are usually more self-conscious and self-involved when they audition than when they perform. They are listening to themselves, watching themselves. And they sometimes overlook their characters' relationships with the other characters in the scene. Or they think of these relationships in a superficial way: the other character is my husband or wife, my lover, my friend, my boss, my mother, father, sister, or child. Relationships can be like diamonds in a goldfish bowl: their value is right in front of you, but you don't see them. Don't take a relationship for granted. Find the *heat* in the relationship, the specific elements that make it emotionally charged. Is it a caring or conflicted relationship? Is it passionate, hostile, or dependent?

At your audition, you will be reading your character's part with someone with whom you have never rehearsed, someone you have never even met before, who reads the lines of the other characters in the scene. So it is crucial that you focus on the specifics of your relationship with the other characters in the scene when you are rehearsing by yourself. You might endow another character in the scene with something that is very real for you: a physical feature, what she wears, how she looks, how she smells, etc. At your audition, you can then endow the reader with this element, which will give you a palpable connection to the reader's character.

If your relationships in the scene suggest a larger context, imagine them in an archetypal way: cat and mouse, child and parent, teacher and student, lawyer and client, lover and lover, lover and ex-lover, doctor and patient, angel and devil, detective and suspect, priest and confessor, etc. Or they may remind you of other characters' relationships in dramatic literature. Thinking in these terms may give you a framework for the scene that will ignite your acting choices.

Ask the questions: What do I want to do to my partner in

the scene? What do I want from my partner? Is my partner the obstacle to my objective? Is my partner helping me achieve my objective?

A scene might center around a relationship with someone who is not in the scene. We cannot imagine playing Juliet without incorporating Juliet's relationship to Romeo in her scenes with her mother, the nurse, and the friar, and in her soliloquies. That relationship conditions all of her actions and behavior. Be sure to invest those relationships outside the scene as fully and as specifically as you do the characters in the scene.

You will learn a great deal about your own character, and the story or event in the scene, from his or her relationships with the other characters, whether they are in the scene, referred to, or fantasized.

8. Where are the "moments" in the scene?

Finding distinctive or significant moments in the scene will ensure that you don't invest every line with equal importance or weight. (A moment can last for a line, a few lines, a pause, or a literal moment.) Choose the moments that illuminate the scene or the character. They might be transitions, humorous moments, climactic moments, etc. The more you *experience* the scene rather than just analyze it, the more the moments will leap out at you.

Always try to find a climactic moment in the scene, if there is one.

Transitions can be particularly exciting moments because we see a change *happening;* you experience something that leads you to another place emotionally or psychologically. These may be very subtle shifts.

Moments can manifest themselves in movement or behavior. *Look for the possibility of humor in every scene.* If the scene is a comedy, select the most important humorous moments. Whatever humor, wit, sarcasm, or irony there is in the scene should be used to reveal character, event, or relationships. Actors are often hired because they have found the humor in the scene and played it well. The reverse is also true!

You should identify *where* the moments happen but not plan exactly *how* you will play them. Deciding on how you will play the moments can lead you into a mechanical performance. You don't know exactly how you will feel at the time of the audition; you should have room to be spontaneous and improvisational. But knowing *where* the moments are will give you a form or structure for your acting choices.

9. *What is the atmosphere of the scene?*

We usually associate atmosphere with a place, a season, a time of day, or an event. Imagine a funeral in a church in winter; a walk on a spring morning through a meadow; a hospital emergency room at 3 A.M. on a holiday weekend; sitting in front of a fire in a cabin on an autumn evening. Imagining these atmospheres arouses your senses. There is no plot and no dialogue, but you would instinctively move, speak, and behave differently in each atmosphere.

The moment the curtain is raised in a theater, you sense something about the play from the set, the lighting, and perhaps the music. You may not be able to describe the atmosphere, but it is there. Once the actors begin to speak and move, the atmosphere is either sustained, heightened, or changed, but it remains an active participant in the play. An atmosphere is created in films or television by the images on the screen and the background music and sound effects from the time the film or show begins.

Can we use atmosphere in an audition? If the scene itself provides an atmosphere—for example, King Lear on the heath with cataracts and hurricanes—it will trigger your sensory resources and inspire your acting. However, you are not often given an atmosphere as powerful as the one in *King Lear*. Frequently, the actual setting of an audition scene is uninspiring: an office, a living room, a park bench, etc.

However, there is another kind of imagined atmosphere that does not depend on the actual setting of the scene, but instead reflects what happens in the scene. *It supports and feeds your acting choices. You might think of it as the landscape in which you are acting.*

Let's say a scene takes place in an office where you know you are about to be fired. The atmosphere of the event feels dangerous to your character. What does a dangerous atmosphere bring to mind? Allow your senses to go that place. A walk on a dark street late at night? Standing on a cliff? Listen to the atmosphere. Feel it on your skin. Suddenly you imagine your heart beating faster, your breath becoming shorter, a sensation of caution occurs. You have made a connection with the acting landscape of the scene, which affects your state of being. There is no need to exhibit or indicate behavior. *But an awareness of the sensory aspect of your character will bring the character to life.*

Playing *against* the atmosphere can be an active choice if it works for the scene and the character. For example, in the same scene and atmosphere just described, you could choose to appear as though you didn't expect to be fired and start the scene in a light-hearted way. It still has the same sensory effect on you, but you are covering your awareness of the danger.

We have all experienced many atmospheres that inspire different kinds of sensory responses: a certain place where you feel totally at ease, another where you feel intimidated, another where you feel a sense of solemnity, another where you feel a sense of anticipation, heights where you feel you're in danger. (The place that feels dangerous to one actor may not feel the same to another.)

The atmosphere can be broken down and connected to objects, sounds, or smells. For example, if the atmosphere feels like a spiritual one, you might imagine a candle burning in a church, or the smell of incense burning in the censer, or the sound of chanting in a temple. If the atmosphere feels like a party, you might imagine champagne bubbling in your mouth, or gay dance music, or blowing on a noisemaker.

When preparing a scene, does the atmosphere feel comfortable, dangerous, spiritual, sensual, suffocating, liberating, secretive, bright, lonely, hot, cold, romantic, silent, dark, noisy, intimate, etc.? You can use the actual atmosphere and/or the acting atmosphere. Then find your connection to that atmosphere, a place, time, or event that arouses your senses and makes you feel alive and present in the scene. *Be sure you are not bringing a different reality to the scene, connected to an emotional event, that might lead you in the wrong direction.*

Using atmosphere as a resource is your secret weapon. The auditors will feel that your audition has extra texture and dimension, but they won't know its source.

10. What is the pre-beat?

A pre-beat is a preparatory moment immediately before you start your audition, in which you gather your concentration and focus. This preparation is a ritual for most athletes. Watch a gymnast before her routine or a baseball pitcher before the pitch. You see them center their energy. When you, the actor, focus your energy in a particular way, you will have a springboard into the scene, an impulse that starts the flow of creative energy that leads you into the scene. When you begin well, you start a chain reaction; one full moment leads to another. If you start to speak without a pre-beat, you might feel you are "not there," which can debilitate you for the rest of the audition.

What often happens at an audition is that you are distracted or thrown off your game. You walk into a new space and see the auditors lined up in theater seats or behind a table, waiting to evaluate your appropriateness for the role. Your name is announced. Nerves rush in. Your courage fails. Your concentration on the scene rushes out. You start speaking your lines and you don't sound anything like you did when you were rehearsing. You were acting well at home, speaking in the character's voice, experiencing the moments, feeling that you were going to get this part. What happened?

Without the pre-beat, your initial focus is apt to be on the event of being judged. A pre-beat changes that focus. It cuts through your nerves and intimidation. It should be chosen and rehearsed at home when you are working on the material, and called upon as a warm-up while you are waiting in the reception room or backstage. *The most provocative element of your pre-beat can be tapped into three or four seconds before you begin the scene.*

The pre-beat should trigger an energy source in the scene. It can be a character element, objective, obstacle, atmosphere, relationship, or the previous moment. It can combine any of these elements. How does the body respond to the energy source? Does that source arouse a physical sensation? If so, it will stimulate you in an immediate way and will connect mind and body.

A good choice for a provocative element to tap into at the audition itself is an affecting image. Images are a way of short-circuiting more complicated mental processes. Images will give you an immediate charge, which will open the door to whatever your acting choice may be.

Objective is a powerful pre-beat, since it arouses your will and is frequently the driving force in the scene. As I mentioned earlier, if you find an objective with high stakes, it may suggest a larger-than-life physical gesture to you, e.g. seduce, shake, eviscerate, embrace, dominate, etc. Imagining the gesture and a sound or words accompanying it, will immediately bring the objective into your body. (Stanislavsky said physicalization of the role affects the actor emotionally more than any other factor. Imagining the physicalization will have the same effect.)

Imagine what the character is wearing. This will enliven the pre-beat because it instantly changes your body. If the play is a period piece, for a woman, it might be a corset, a bustle, or a cape; for a man, it might be a hat, gloves, or boots. Imagining the costume may not be enough, but it can be combined with other energy sources.

An awareness of how the character breathes at the top of the scene can be helpful. A breath may be shallow or deep, long or short, swallowed or free-flowing, but it will bring you inside the body of the character. (Some changes in breath will happen naturally as you are playing the scene. Try to be aware of this connection with your breath as you prepare at home, as it may change your inner rhythm and put you in a different gear.)

Morris Carnovsky, actor and teacher, suggested a preparation (or pre-beat) which he called "The Cry." It is a phrase or paraphrase that the character might be thinking just before the scene begins. It could be invented or it might be a line from the script. He used an example from *The Winter's Tale*, when Hermione is falsely charged with adultery by her husband, Leontes, and is about to be tried. Her cry is "How could you?" repeated two or three times in the imagination. It is at once a question and an accusation, and contains the pain and frustration and anguish she is experiencing. It calls forth all the elements that Hermione needs to begin the scene.

Experiment with a cry aloud when you're rehearsing at home. It is helpful to repeat it many times, perhaps in different ways. Try several different cries until you find the one that stirs your spirit. Sometimes, the cry is a sound rather than words, a sound that expresses the inner feeling of the character at that particular moment.

A strong pre-beat has a big payoff. Without the pre-beat, you make the auditors wait for you to warm up during your audition, or to get to that moment on the second page where you show your talent. By that time, they are much less interested than they would have been had you started off with a strong attack.

Be inventive in finding your pre-beat. But whatever you do, don't start from zero.

A preacher on television, speaking to his congregation, said, "I must leap into the text, I must be one with the text, I must smell the aroma of the text, then I can preach."

And then you can audition.

Chapter IV

———————

APPLYING ACTABLE

CHOICES

Asking the ten actable choice questions will provide a way for you to explore and animate the scene. Even though in any particular scene some of the actable choice questions may not apply as much as others, addressing them all as possibilities will resonate in the audition.

Before you work on your scene, ask yourself, "What interests me about this character? What do I like about her?" *Find something that attracts you to the character*, that will connect you to the material and focus your acting choices.

When you read the scene for the first time, you may have a very strong intuitive response. You feel you know just what you want to do with the material. Nonetheless, read the scene over and over again, asking *all* the actable choice questions. See what else your imagination bumps into in the course of rereading the scene. The answers should enrich what you're doing, or focus your work in a better way, or fill in a moment more specifically.

As you read the scene, make a note of any image, key word, or short phrase that triggers an impulse or idea. (I call these "trigger words.") Write your notes in pencil, because they are likely to change as you work. Don't reject ideas that come to you out of order. Take them as they come!

Reread the whole scene regularly *to yourself* during your preparation. When working on separate sections or moments, it's easy to lose the feeling of the whole.

I like to think about an audition scene right after I wake up in the morning, while I'm still in bed and not fully awake. Images come to mind that are uncensored by my intellect. Sometimes, I can get a feeling for the scene and the character that is fresh and surprising.

SCENE ANALYSIS

Here is how I would apply actable choices to prepare an audition for the role of Anne in *A Little Night Music,* a musical play by Hugh Wheeler and Stephen Sondheim. I have not seen the whole script. I have been told only that the play is set in Sweden around 1900, and that in the scene that follows, which I have been asked to prepare, Anne is nineteen and Fredrika is thirteen.

ANNE

[*Off*] Henrik!

HENRIK

Oh God! There she is!
[*He runs off*]

ANNE

[*Off*] Henrik, dear!

FREDRIKA

[*Calls after him*]: Mr. Egerman! Please don't do anything rash!
[*Anne runs on*]

FREDRIKA

Oh, Mrs. Egerman, I'm so terribly worried.

ANNE

You poor dear. What about?

FREDRIKA

About Mr. Egerman—Junior, that is.

ANNE

Silly Henrik! I was just coming out to scold him.

FREDRIKA

I am so afraid he may do himself an injury.

ANNE

How delightful to be talking to someone younger than myself. No doubt he has been denouncing the wickedness of the world—and quoting Martin Luther? Dearest Fredrika, all you were witnessing was the latest crisis in his love affair with God.

FREDRIKA

Not with God, Mrs. Egerman—with you!

ANNE

[*Totally surprised*]
Me!

FREDRIKA

You may not have noticed, but he is madly, hopelessly in love with you.

ANNE

Is that really the truth?

FREDRIKA

Yes, he told me so himself.

ANNE

[*Thrilled, flattered, perhaps more*]
The poor dear boy! How ridiculous of him—and yet how charming. Dear friend, if you knew how insecure I constantly

feel, how complicated the marriage state seems to be. I adore old Fredrik of course, but . . .

FREDRIKA

[*Interrupting*]
But Mrs. Egerman, he ran down towards the lake!

ANNE

[*Laughing*]
To gaze over the ornamental waters! How touching! Let us go and find him. [*Anne takes Fredrika's arm and starts walking off with her*] Such a good looking boy, isn't he? Such long, long lashes . . .
[*They exit, giggling, arm-in-arm*]

Here is how I would apply the actable choices to this scene:

1. *Intuitive response:*

My first impression is of a world where there is a sense of propriety. The scene feels very romantic. Anne sounds like she's trying to act like an older woman. In the course of the scene, it feels as though Anne drops the veil covering her feelings. I imagine a formal garden in the late afternoon. Anne and Henrik remind me of Romeo and Juliet—forbidden lovers.

2. *World of the play:*

My image of Anne is that she is corseted, both literally and figuratively. She wears perfume that smells of roses. Her full, long skirt rustles as she moves; perhaps it is taffeta or silk. Fredrika wears a straw hat with a flower in it. Both Anne and Fredrika sound educated and upper class.

3. *What is it about?*

The given circumstances are that Anne is married to Fredrik, an older man. In the scene, she finds out from a younger woman, Fredrika, that her stepson, Henrik, is in love with her and they go off to find him. The beginning section is "Where is Henrik?" The middle, "He loves me." And the last, "I love him!" Since the end of the scene is always inherent in its beginning in some way, the stage direction "(Thrilled, flattered, perhaps more)" clues me into Anne's inner passion for Henrik, which gives me a strong focus before my entrance.

4. *Character:*

If I look for similarities between Anne and me, I can identify with her romanticism and passion. There are many differences between us; I don't have her mocking humor or her impulsiveness. Her walk and her gestures are very feminine and have a faster tempo than mine, as does her speech.

5. *Objective:*

Although Anne tells Fredrika she wants to scold Henrik, I think she enters the scene wanting to flirt with him or perhaps comfort him. (He seems to have done something that he feels upset about). Anne's action in the first section could be to mock Henrik to Fredrika so as to mask her feelings for him. In the second section she wants to open her heart to Fredrika. In the last section, I would raise the stakes: she wants to give herself to Henrik.

6. Obstacle:

Anne's main obstacle is her need to maintain her role as stepmother. Anne must not allow her interest in Henrik to be apparent to Fredrika. In the second section, Anne's ability to resist her love for Henrik begins to break down. By the third section, she has virtually dropped her stepmother guise.

7. Relationship:

Three relationships define Anne in the scene.

The first is with Fredrik: I don't know how old Fredrik really is, but I want to create a contrast between Henrik and Fredrik, so I think of him as a much older man who snores and has bad teeth and nose hairs. The image fortifies my desire for Henrik.

The second relationship is with Henrik. Henrik is Prince Charming, adorable and sexy. In my youth, a young man I was infatuated with left me gifts of little white stones he found on the beach. A white stone, or something like it, in my pocket at the audition, or in my imagination, might evoke romantic feelings.

The third relationship is with Fredrika. During the scene, Anne's relationship with Fredrika changes radically. At the beginning of the scene, Anne speaks to her as though she were a child, somewhat condescendingly, and by the end of the scene, Fredrika has become a trusted friend and confidante.

8. *Moments:*

I choose to focus on three significant acting moments in the scene. When Anne enters, she finds Fredrika instead of Henrik, and she must rise above Fredrika's concerns, which she does with humor and frivolity—"Silly Henrik!" etc. In the climatic moment when Anne exclaims "Me!", she begins to drop the veil covering her feelings. And when she decides to go and find Henrik, she throws caution to the wind and reveals her undisguised admiration and attraction for him—"Such long, long lashes . . ."

9. *Atmosphere:*

The atmosphere of the countryside adds to the romantic feeling of the scene. I imagine a beautiful garden and green rolling hills. The air is sweet and balmy. However, the acting atmosphere for Anne is also dangerous, because she has come out to be alone with her stepson. If I imagine the scene taking place in the evening, the danger would be heightened.

10. *Pre-beat:*

What would best prepare me for my entrance? I imagine that, to prepare for her meeting with Henrik, Anne puts perfume behind her ears and on her wrists, and perhaps in her cleavage. Since her objective is dangerous and romantic, she feels warm and aroused, her underarms are damp with sweat. She feels her heart pumping, which will affect my awareness of my breath. Henrik's eyelashes inspire me. And there are the white stones. The energy connected with my objective will help me play the first section with Fredrika in a heightened way.

LOSING ISAIAH

Here is how I would apply actable choices to the role of Kadar Lewis, a male African-American lawyer in a scene from the movie *Losing Isaiah*.

[Exterior: store-front law office, Brooklyn—night]
[Selma stands in front of the low brick building in her best Sunday clothes. They're old but clean. The lettering on the glass store front identifies it as THE COMMUNITY LAW SERVICES *office. Old venetian blinds hang half open in the window. Graffiti is spray-painted on the brick. She enters.]*

[Interior law office—night]
[The reception area is empty. No one sits at the switchboard. The clock reads 6:45. She tries a door. It's locked. She is turning to go when a tall, slim black man in shirt sleeves pushes open another door into the reception area. This is KADAR LEWIS, thirties.]

LEWIS

Ms. Richards?
[*Selma nods.*]

LEWIS

The office is closed.

SELMA

I couldn't get off work. The lady I work for, she's a lawyer, too, and she was late. An' I couldn't leave Dana . . .

LEWIS

Follow me.
[*He turns toward the door. Selma follows*]

[*Interior law office—night*]
[*A large room is partitioned into offices by wallboard dividers. Lewis enters one of them. Selma follows.*]

[*Interior Lewis's office—night*]
[*The floor is covered with piles of briefs. Books and papers are everywhere. There's an old leather couch in one corner and two facing wooden chairs. Nothing matches. A pile of clothing is heaped in one of the chairs. Selma hesitates as Lewis takes a seat in the other chair, picking up some papers and a pad as he does so.*]

LEWIS

Have a seat.

[*She looks around, sees a clear spot, and, pushing aside some papers, sits in a corner of the leather couch. She waits as Lewis looks over the papers in front of him.*]

SELMA

I ain't never seen a black lawyer.

LEWIS

I understand that you'd like to reinstate your parental rights.
[*Selma says nothing. These words have passed over her head.*]

LEWIS

You gave your child up for adoption. Now you want him back.

SELMA

No, sir.

LEWIS

You don't want him back?

SELMA

No, I didn't give him up for adoption.

LEWIS

You left him in an alley. You abandoned him, Ms. Richards. That's the same thing.

SELMA

I was a junkie.

LEWIS

[*severe*]
And now?

SELMA

And now I'm not.

LEWIS

How long have you been . . .

SELMA

Clean. Past a year.

LEWIS

Then why haven't you tried to claim your child before this?
Why did you let your rights lapse?

SELMA

I thought he was dead.

LEWIS

Dead?

SELMA

I was stoned. I left him . . . outside . . .

LEWIS

But you've been through rehab and you're working now.

SELMA

I take care of Dana for Mrs. Fredericks, like I told you.
[He writes something on the legal pad. She watches.]

SELMA

You don't like me much.

LEWIS

I don't like what put you in this situation, Ms. Richards.

SELMA

You don't have to talk down to me. I can pay.

LEWIS

There's no fee involved here.

SELMA

I don't want charity.

LEWIS

We take on cases we consider to be socially relevant, Ms. Richards. If we win them, they set legal precedent. Your case fits that profile. The fee is covered by donations. *[looking through a file]* Your child is living with a white family. They have almost completed adoption proceedings. We can try to get your parental rights restored, but it's not going to be easy. These people have money. They're white. They've treated him well. You abandoned him. You were a junkie and you're black.

SELMA

But I'm his mother.

LEWIS

I'm sure Mrs. Lewin feels fairly strongly right now, that she is. And there are a lot of people who will agree with her.

SELMA

But you'll help me?

LEWIS

. . . I'll help you.
[*A beat of silence.*]

SELMA

You think I have a chance?

LEWIS

I really don't know. This is a white world and we're black. They make the rules.

1. *Intuitive:*

Lewis reminds me of a death-penalty lawyer I know in the South, working against great odds. Lewis is a deeply moral public-interest lawyer, who denies himself money and power. He is in the law office alone after everyone else has left; he seems committed and overworked. He wants to help Selma but is tough on her. He clearly understands the social ills that contributed to her condition, but he disapproves of her prior actions. In taking on her case, his sense of injustice supersedes all other considerations.

2. *World of the play:*

The description of the Brooklyn storefront and the office inside give me a vivid idea of the poor neighborhood and the public-interest nature of Lewis's practice. The messy office suggests that Lewis has a massive amount of work. I imagine phones ringing all day long and people crowding in for legal help. He probably shares a secretary with many other lawyers. I imagine the smell of stale food from half-eaten sandwiches and paper cups half full of cold coffee scattered on his desk. I see Lewis in a shirt with a worn collar, slightly stained from eating at his desk while talking on the phone.

3. *What is the scene about?:*

The given circumstances: Selma is an ex-junkie who abandoned her baby while she was stoned. She has since been rehabilitated and, in this scene, tries to get legal help to retrieve her child from the white couple who has been taking care of him and succeeds in getting Lewis a public-interest lawyer to help her. The beginning section is "Discovery," the middle section is "Straight talk," and the last section is "I'm on your side."

4. *Character*:

If I look for similarities between Lewis and me, I identify with his desire to fight for Selma's rights. However, I need to rachet up my own willingness to sacrifice for her cause. As for the differences between us, he has the mind of a lawyer, quicker and more knowledgeable than mine, and clearly he's much tougher than I would be in similar circumstances.

5. *Objective*:

Lewis states that his overall objective is "to set a legal precedent." But that doesn't incite me. A more active overall objective might be "to unite the baby with his mother." In the first section, his action is to test Selma, to challenge her, and to discover if she is truly off drugs. (Can he count on her in court?) In the second section, he wants to shake her up so she knows what she's up against: "They're white. They've treated him well. You abandoned him. You were a junkie and you're black." And in the third section, which starts with Selma's question, "But you'll help me?", he wants to reassure her and join her in her fight for her child.

6. *Obstacle:*

Selma presents an obstacle to Lewis: she is uneducated, an ex-junkie, and did a terrible thing. He is fighting his own disapproval of her. The larger obstacle is what he's up against: "This is a white world and we're black. They make the rules." A more immediate physical obstacle could be that he is hungry and tired after a long, busy day.

7. *Relationships:*

I think his underlying relationship with Selma is a sympathetic one, even though he disapproves of her. Selma represents many of the societal ills that Lewis is fighting against: poverty, drugs, poor education, loss of parental rights, etc.

8. *Moments:*

My first moment will be the pause just before Lewis says "Follow me" in the first section. She's late, it's after-hours, he'd rather not see her but decides to bring her in. Why? Perhaps Lewis is a man who finds it very difficult to refuse anyone in trouble. Or there may be something about Selma that affects him.

Another moment could be the line "I don't like what put you in this situation, Ms. Richards." He is making it clear that his feelings are objective, not personal, perhaps saying it for his own benefit as well as hers, trying to overcome his disapproval.

I see the third moment in the pause before Lewis says, "I'll help you." This is not an easy decision. Here, I would soften my attitude toward her for the first time in the scene, and continue that attitude through Lewis's last line. This change in his attitude toward Selma creates a polarity for him from the beginning of the scene.

9. *Atmosphere*:

The description of the storefront and the office help me imagine the informal, messy atmosphere in which Lewis works. He feels at home here and it provides him with the opportunity to get his work done. It's a comfortable atmosphere for Lewis. But the stakes in the scene are very high, and the odds are enormous. So my acting landscape is deadly serious and businesslike.

10. *Pre-Beat*:

I have been waiting for Selma. I imagine Selma's African-American child in the arms of a white mother. That image gives me the reason to be here in this place at this time. I look for a connection to Lewis's physical state of being. I go to the physical obstacles: hunger and tiredness. The sensation of emptiness in my stomach sharpens my irritation with Selma's lateness and my disapproval of her in the first section. My shoulders and neck may be slightly bent from fatigue, though I try not to show it.

MY WILDEST DREAMS

Here is a scene from a sitcom, *My Wildest Dreams*. I am auditioning for the role of Sheldon Brighton.

[*Interior classroom—morning*]
[*A typical kids' classroom. Maps and a large poster of Barney adorn the walls. Lisa is sitting uncomfortably in a student's desk. Sheldon walks in on her. Sheldon is Josh's teacher. Sheldon's a "sensitive guy," (disgustingly) earnest. He still lives in the sixties.*]

SHELDON

Ms. James. Well, this is very special for me. I love sitting down and bonding with the parents of my kids. May I call you by your first name?

LISA

Sure; I'm Lisa.
[*Sheldon sits at his desk*]

SHELDON

And you may call me Sheldon. And your husband is . . . ?

LISA

Working. He's working and watching our baby. You called me in here because there's some trouble with my son?

SHELDON

We don't like to use the expression "trouble" here. We prefer the term "misdirection." I have very sensitive antennae that tunes into children and I find that Michael—

LISA

Josh.

SHELDON

Josh. Of course. I'm finding that Josh isn't meeting certain motivational goals. When I come across this kind of challenge, I call the parent in to query as to whether there is an environmental problem.

LISA

Are you saying that Josh isn't learning the things you're teaching?

SHELDON

Teaching. Teaching. That's a word I like to avoid. I don't teach; rather, I inform. I work with the child to bring out the child within the child, and what I have found is that if there is a problem with the child at school . . .
[*Sheldon leans over and whispers knowingly, meaningfully*]

SHELDON

It means there is a problem with the child at home. Could that be a possibility?

LISA

Gee, I really don't know. I mean I only got out of the drunk tank yesterday. I was doing alright after I left rehab, but then my husband got busted for armed robbery and we made bail, but then when he got home he went crazy because my lover is living in the house, well, in the basement actually, he's a chemist, but if you called me in here to grill me about my personal life instead of telling me like a human being what's wrong with my kid . . .

SHELDON

Lisa. Lisa. I can't help but sense some hostility here. It's just that your son Michael—

LISA

Josh!

SHELDON

Of course. Josh, isn't doing his homework. That's all. That's why I wanted to chat.

1. Intuitive response:

Child-rearing advice that advocates great care in the way you behave with children so as not to traumatize them has been taken to an extreme. From his first line, Sheldon uses pretentious words such as "bonding," "misdirection," "motivational goals," and "query" that clue me in to his character. And, of course, his name is Sheldon *Brighton!* If I look for something that interests me about Sheldon, it is his treatment of Lisa—as though she is one of his students.

2. *World of the play:*

Since the classroom is described as having maps and a poster of Barney, I imagine it to be a second- or third-grade classroom, so the children would be about seven or eight years old. I see Sheldon in a bright red or purple shirt and a bow tie that maintains an up atmosphere in his classroom. Sheldon's world is clearly at odds with Lisa's world from the get-go.

3. *What is the scene about?:*

Sheldon has called Lisa in to discuss the fact that her son, Josh, is not doing his homework. (*How* Sheldon discusses it defines the scene.) Here is how I would name the sections: the first section is "Bonding," the second, "What are you doing wrong, Lisa?" and the third, "Naughty girl!"

4. *Character:*

Looking for similarities, I remember when my first child was three years old, I worried I was making mistakes that would affect her in negative ways, and went to a child psychologist to get advice. My need to behave according to accepted theories of child psychology connects me in some way to Sheldon. If I didn't have that history, I might think of a different situation, in which I felt I always had the right answers and everybody else was wrong. The writer's description of Sheldon clues me in: "a 'sensitive guy' (disgustingly) earnest." The differences between Sheldon and me are that Sheldon seems self-important and condescending. He doesn't listen, he corrects.

5. Objective:

I think his objective is to uncover the dirt at Lisa's home. His action is to dazzle her with his sensitivity to children.

6. Obstacle:

She may not want to admit there are any problems at home.

7. Relationship:

He patronizes Lisa. I get the feeling he talks to every parent the same way. This is his "script." He can't even remember Josh's name, so he probably relates to the children using another "script."

8. Moments:

I would choose the following three moments. The first moment occurs when Sheldon corrects Lisa. "We don't like to use the expression 'trouble' here." She becomes his student, which establishes the relationship. The second moment occurs when he says, "It means there is a problem with the child at home. Could that be a possibility?" The stage direction is that "Sheldon leans over and whispers knowingly, meaningfully." In this case, I would follow the stage direction; it will be

fun to play and, since he is blaming her, very much in character. The third moment is a reaction to Lisa's monologue about
the drunk tank, when Sheldon finally "gets" Lisa, acknowledges her hostility and says innocently, "Josh isn't doing his
homework. That's all."

9. Atmosphere:

Sheldon feels very cozy in the classroom atmosphere he has
created. The acting atmosphere is also comfortable for him,
though Lisa is anything but comfortable in the scene. I think
what makes the scene funny is that he refuses to allow her to
break into his atmosphere.

10. Pre-beat:

Sheldon's need to dazzle Lisa charges me up. I think he's
excited everytime he has the opportunity to impress a new parent. And the purple shirt and bowtie add to the dazzle.

My take on the scenes serves only as an example of how I
would apply the actable choices. You may have different ideas
that work for you. Creative individuality is what acting is all
about.

Preparation should never be cast in stone. You will be
affected by the circumstances of the audition, often in wonderful ways. Performance energy rushes in, and your impulses
in the moment may take you somewhere other than where you
have been before. Once you are grounded in the scene, you
should feel confident enough to respond to those impulses.

Chapter V

———

AUDITIONING FOR

THE CAMERA

There are important differences between acting on stage and acting for the camera. Those differences should affect how you audition for one or the other.

At a theater audition, the director looks for your potential to play a role; she knows your final performance will evolve from your mutual collaboration during the rehearsal period. When you audition for the camera, the director looks at you through a different glass. What you show at your audition for film or television is what the director expects to see, more or less, when you appear on the set.

If you have never worked in film or television, you may be shocked to learn that, apart from a rehearsal for camera blocking, as a general rule you will have little or no rehearsal with the director and the other actors. (A television series, or a film or television show where you have a major role, are the exceptions to the rule.) The director's main focus is not on the actors, but instead on the complicated technical aspects of film making. The director will edit your performance, but chances are you will get little or no direction on the set to help you interpret your role. So be grateful if you have a director who talks to you about your character and helps you enrich your performance. There are a few.

A film is a story told primarily with images. Alfred Hitchcock said he always tried to tell as much of the story as possible without words: "Words belong to literature." *The audience registers what they see before they take in what they hear.*

A play is a story told primarily with words. On the stage, actors must project their voices and convey emotion by broad gestures and physical movement; a raised eyebrow or a hushed whisper will not read past the first row. What you say and how you say it are the primary vehicles for expression. Stage actors must learn to project their voices and pick up their cues.

If you have trained for the theater, does this mean that to act for the camera you have to throw out everything you've spent years learning and perfecting? A resounding NO! The outer manifestation of your work is different, but the acting process is the same. Actable choices can serve as a guide for camera work as well as for theater.

When you audition in front of the camera, you will usually be in a medium close-up, sitting or standing still. You may ask, "How can I bring life to my work when I am confined in this way? When auditioning for the theater, I may choose not to move, but at least I have the freedom to move if I want to." The answer is that the camera reveals what is happening inside your mind, heart, and body; what you are thinking, feeling, and wishing. Your acting sources are the same as they would be if you were able to move. Use the auditioning space as though you were in the character's environment, as you would on the stage. When you look out, imagine a window, a field, or whatever.

If you have a theatrical background, you may not feel like you are acting when you are in front of the camera. Acting on the stage is not only a psychological and emotional experience; it is also a physical experience. You use your voice and body in a heightened way. *Camera work requires a different balance between your inner life and its outer expression.* Your performance should reflect your acting choices but needs to be contained.

CONTAINMENT

If you are a stage actor and have ever had to project your voice to the top of the balcony when you were playing an intimate scene, you will find containment a luxury. *The camera loves intimacy.* At a camera audition, there is no need to heighten your physical or verbal expression. Your voice should not be as "present," either in vocal energy or articulation, as it is when you are onstage. You can speak and behave naturally, conversationally. It is as though you were sitting across a small table, talking in your natural speaking voice.

Alexa Fogel, casting director and producer, says, "Don't overemphasize in auditioning for the camera. You will interrupt the flow of the scene by worrying whether I get it or not. If you are playing a physical distance greater than three to four feet (from the reader), the scene will appear overemphasized or the-atrical. It is the equivalent of playing to the back of the house."

Your eyes are your most valuable asset. The camera reads your thoughts and feelings through your eyes. Looking directly at the reader, looking away, the rhythm of your looks, the quality of your looks, have more impact than any other element in camera audi-tioning in a medium close-up.

You may have a scene for the camera where you feel like screaming from irritation or joy or anger. If you were actually shooting the scene on a set, the level of your voice would be adjusted by the sound engineer. But there is no sound engi-neer at your audition. You have to find an adjustment that allows you to express yourself without screaming. You can cer-tainly raise your voice, but you need to develop a sense of what is too much. Everything is magnified in a medium close-up, so a little goes a long way.

BEHAVIOR

In camera work, the primary vehicle for communication is your behavior, not the words in the script; your actions or reac-tions while you're talking and while you're *not* talking.

Turn off the sound when you are watching television or

movies at home, just to observe the actors' behavior. Go to a foreign film and ignore the subtitles. Watch real people being interviewed on television, people who are behaving in real life. *Notice how people communicate without using words.*

Behavior is in small gestures or slight changes of expression. Less is indeed more in front of the camera. Your mind and body intuitively work together. If you are imagining something or experiencing sensations, thoughts, and feelings, we see them without your showing us. In life, you don't think about how your face moves or doesn't move when you think or feel things, it just happens. As you work in front of the camera, you will become more sensitive to your nonverbal impulses. Open yourself to those impulses and they will lead you to natural behavior.

I once heard a television director say to an actor, "Give it more air." He wanted the actor to loosen up his speech, sometimes referred to as "muddying it up." Since the camera is telling the story primarily through images, you can take the time to allow words or thoughts to germinate, to express themselves in lifelike behavior that will register on camera. At your audition, since the camera is only on you, you can overlap the other person's lines, a luxury generally not permitted on the set for editing reasons.

LISTENING

Listening in front of the camera is as important as speaking, perhaps more important. Often an actor will be very animated when he is speaking, but virtually dead while listening to the reader. Study the lines of the other character in the scene carefully when you are rehearsing for the audition. Know what he is saying. What are you thinking and experiencing while your partner speaks? Don't be a zombie and wait until your partner finishes his lines before you begin to react. *The way you listen is an acting choice.*

Readers at taped auditions sit or stand very close to one side of the camera. Since the microphone is on the camera, the readers sometimes tend to speak very softly. Tell them if you can't hear them!—Don't make do.

It is frequently appropriate to listen without looking at the other character in the scene, and often more interesting and true to life. This is crucial in auditioning for the camera. When you turn away or shift your gaze, we feel that something is cooking. Don't be mechanical about looking away from your partner; follow your impulses. *Develop your sense of when it is important to focus directly on your partner and when it is not.* If you were playing the role on the set, the camera would move back and forth between you and the reader at different angles, and there would be great variety in the visual points of view. However, at your audition, we look at you from only one point of view, so your choice of how you listen can make the scene more or less interesting.

Actors who have trained for theater need to be aware of the need for this adjustment. On the stage, you learn to be quite still when another actor is speaking, so that the audience stays focused on him or her. By contrast, in auditioning for the camera, your reaction to the speaker tells us what is happening in the scene.

It is sometimes hard to respond appropriately at an audition if you have a reader who reads his lines without any sense of their meaning. In that case, listen to *what* he is saying, not *how*. This will be easier if you have studied the other characters' lines in advance. If you are too nervous or distracted to listen with all your attention, you may find it helpful to write down key words or phrases on your script that synthesize what the other character is saying or what you're thinking while he's talking. So, if you're unable to fully "hear" the reader, you will know what he's saying and can respond truthfully. This may help you stay in the scene.

If you are not familiar with the script, you may be reading the other character's lines rather than listening and responding while the reader is speaking. Don't. The auditors need to see your face, not the top of your head. If you are dependent on the script, it is better to listen to your partner, and then take a moment if you need to to look down at the script, staying in character throughout. The script should be held up, out of frame, not on your lap, so you don't have to bend your head all the way down in order to read it. (Use the scanning technique I discuss in Chapter VIII.) Don't pretend to listen, while thinking about when to look down at the script for your next line. (A glazed expression will give you away.)

SPONTANEITY

Good acting for the camera must have an improvisational quality.
Spontaneity is key to screen acting, be it film or television. We
have to believe that what you are doing and saying is truthful
and happening for the first time, that you are entirely present
in the moment. (In theory, since the material is still fresh, it
should be easier to be spontaneous when auditioning.)

Preparing your audition using actable choices will ground
you in the who, what, and how of the scene. You can then go
into the audition confidently, and trust yourself to act spontaneously.

You must have seen film or television performances that are
so fresh, intuitive, and unpredictable that it seems as though
the character is inventing the lines on the spot. That is what
makes the world marvel at Marlon Brando and Jimmy Dean.
Lily Taylor in *Mystic Pizza*, Helen Hunt in *As Good As It Gets*,
Daniel Day Lewis in *The Boxer*, Hilary Swank and Chloë
Sevigny in *Boys Don't Cry*, Mark Ruffalo in *You Can Count on
Me*, and Judi Dench in everything, convey that same quality.
In *Tea with Mussolini*, every time Ms. Dench appears, it is as
though the camera catches the character in the middle of a
spontaneous moment—always alive, truthful, spontaneous.
Her technique is seamless.

SPECIFICITY

What is it that makes one line different from the next? Finding
the changes or shifts in the scene (actable choice number
three) will help you discover *what* is happening in the scene
and *where* changes occur. *How* the scene changes will often
arise from choosing your actions (actable choice number four).
It is to your advantage to discover the colors and nuances that
move the scene from moment to moment, all of which the
camera will pick up. *Whatever you do, don't let every line sound
the same.*

MOMENTS

As we discussed in Actable Choices (chapter III), compelling
moments are what interest us most about a performance and
make it memorable.

Here's an example. In the film *City of Angels,* I had a scene
with Nicolas Cage, who was portraying an angel posing as a
human being. In the scene, he was playing with my grand-
daughter, Hannah, and I wanted to take a picture of them. I
said, "Smile, Hannah," to my granddaughter, and Nicolas
Cage, who was looking at the child, slowly raised his head,
turned toward me, almost in slow motion, and stared at my
Polaroid as if he were a deer in headlights. The look incorporated bewilderment and wonder reflecting his fear that an
angel's image might not come out on film (it didn't). I don't

know whether his reaction was spontaneous or planned, but it was chilling. After the film was edited, the moment lasted a tenth of a second but it was still effective.

Compelling moments can happen while you're speaking or during a pause. The pause, however, must never be gratuitous.

Stillness can create a powerful moment in front of the camera. If you have a reason to be still, if it is natural for the character to behave that way at that moment, be still. Stillness can often be more meaningful and have more impact than words and movement. You may be still because you're thinking, absorbing what your partner has just said, or radiating some thought or feeling to your partner.

Margo Jefferson discusses the art of stillness on camera: "What an underrated quality stillness is. It is partly the ability to listen and make listening an action that has consequences for the speaker. And it is partly the ability to ground a scene. When an actor really knows how to be still, we feel her taking in all the other emotions on screen and holding onto them for us, clarifying their meaning."

As discussed earlier, a moment of reaction or behavior opposite to what we expect from the character can be powerful as an acting choice. On camera, it is particularly interesting if your character is saying one thing while thinking another; your thoughts are illuminated by the lens.

GENRES

Soap opera material tends to be melodramatic. Nonetheless, to audition effectively, you must find the truth in your character, your relationships, and the event of the scene. Ellen Novack, former casting director and producer of *One Life to Live,* says, "You can't ride on the words; find a strong subtext, counter to the words. Make an effort to go deeply into material that is not deep, and it will pop open." She describes the soap opera style as "generally intense with an emphasis on emotional responses."

If you're auditioning for sitcoms, sample the current crop and you will get a sense of their style. In most sitcoms, the writers pay close attention to the jokes, which usually come rapid fire. The scripts are punctuated very carefully for comic timing. It will serve you to heed that punctuation. Nothing bad happens that does not get a positive resolution. The lights are bright, the humor is punched up, the characters overreact. But the audience must still believe in the characters. So don't sacrifice authenticity for the jokes. Learn to focus on both, preferably at the same time.

Aisha Coley, who was the casting director on *The Cosby Show,* talks about the difference between sitcoms and comedy shows. She feels actors need to make a distinction between being funny in a natural way, as in *The Cosby Show,* and doing the kind of shtick and one-liners you find in sitcoms. It is an important distinction.

PACE

Timing is crucial in auditioning for the camera. You don't have an editor to make cuts that correct the timing of your scenes. In general, you need to sense how to pick up the pace and not be self-indulgent in elongating moments. However, if you rush through the material and don't give yourself the time to breathe and play truthfully, you may miss the juice of the scene. There are times when cues should be picked up immediately, and times when you should allow your partner's response to land on you before you respond. Practice in front of a camera, then play it back. You should be able to tell when your timing works for the scene and when it doesn't.

In comedy, the pace is faster than in drama. We become aware of the absence of pace in comedy when you lose the energy and humor of the scene. Be sensitive to the rhythm of the material and, at the same time, play the moments. The balance is sometimes difficult to find but important to achieve.

REHEARSAL

When you rehearse at home for your audition, don't start by sitting in a chair. Don't restrict yourself physically. Move around freely while you rehearse. Moving will help you find the rhythm and energy of the character and the scene. If you don't use your body in rehearsing the scene, it will be harder to connect with the mind, emotions, and will of the character.

When you rehearse later in a chair or while standing still, that physicality will be reflected in your posture, your small gestures, and your manner of expression. (Sir Alec Guinness is said to have made large movements in rehearsing for film, but when he was in front of the camera, he hardly moved.) As a student of mine phrased it, "If your body hasn't done it, it doesn't know it!"

TAPING

Most auditions for film or television are taped in the presence of the casting director, and sometimes other auditors are present. Ask the camera operator how the camera will frame you, so you know how large your image will be on the screen and how much freedom of movement you have. Usually, the camera frames you in a medium close-up, from the top of your head to the middle of your chest. Be careful not to move much from side to side, as you will go out of frame. You have a little leeway (a few inches) in movement forward and back. If the camera shoots you from the waist up in a larger frame, you will have more leeway in all directions. While some casting directors will have the camera operator follow you, this is the exception rather than the rule. So when you prepare your audition, assume that you will sit or stand in one position. If you walk into the audition space and see a chair in front of the camera but would rather stand, you can ask if the camera could be moved to accommodate you. Usually no one will object. If you get off to a bad start, you can ask to start again (provided you're not halfway into the scene).

SANS TAPING

Some film auditions are held without a camera; typically, in a small audition room. When I was casting or auditioning for film, Michael Cimino, John Carpenter, Woody Allen, Donald Petrie, James Ivory, Roland Joffé, James Foley, John Sayles, Alan Parker, and Bob Fosse didn't tape actors. Habits and styles change, but there are still some directors who don't tape their auditions.

When I cast for James Ivory, we would usually see actors in a small conference room or office. The actor would sit at a table across from us. Sometimes the actor would ask if he could move around. This was fine with James; his eye is so experienced that he can imagine seeing through the lens without a camera. However, the actor still needs to perform vocally and behaviorally as though he were on camera, though he is not as restricted physically as he would be if he were being taped.

Try to find out in advance if you are going to be taped. It's a good idea to be prepared, one way or another.

SLATE

When you hear "Action," or are given some other signal at your audition, you will be asked to "slate" (say) your name directly into the camera before you begin the audition scene. You should never look directly into the camera, other than when you are saying your name, unless you are directed to do so. I suggest saying your name in a friendly, straightforward fashion, as a means of identification, rather than trying to be coy, charming, or funny. You'd be surprised what some actors try to do when they are saying their names! Too cute!

PRE-BEAT

Don't feel obliged to start speaking as soon as you slate your name. Take a moment (three to four seconds) before you start the scene. This is the time to tap into whatever pre-beat you've prepared in advance. You are in a small room close to the auditors, and it may be harder to concentrate than when you are on a stage or in a large audition space. If you feel tense (usually it hits you between your eyes or in your jaw and neck), take a normal breath with a sensation of openness. This will help release the tension. I find the sensation of openness particularly helpful in auditioning for the camera because it releases you from the inside, even though you are restricted physically. Thinking "feeling of ease" will also help. If you are starting a very emotional scene and need more than three to four seconds, you can ask the camera operator in advance to turn off the camera after the slate so you have an extra few seconds to prepare. You can give a signal when you're ready. (Don't take more than ten to fifteen seconds.)

Acting teacher Ron Burrus suggests that you begin the

scene with a nonverbal moment. A nonverbal moment can be, for example, a small gesture, a slight turn away and back to the reader, a change in breathing, or any behavior that will lead you into the scene. The moment should be very brief, but it will help you establish the character and your state of being before you speak. Ron also suggests ending the scene with a nonverbal moment so you don't break out of the scene the instant you stop speaking.

CROSSING CAMERA

If you choose to turn away from the reader at some point in the scene, turn toward the opposite side of the camera from where the reader is sitting. This is called "crossing camera." If the reader is playing more than one character, you can address all of your lines to her, or turn your head to the other side of the camera to address an imaginary character. If you turn away from your reader in the *other* direction, away from the camera, we will only see the side of your face. It is always better to cross camera, so the camera can get a better view. When you turn away, don't turn a full profile. Even small moves on camera are significant in a medium close-up.

ADJUSTMENTS

After the first take, the casting director or director may give you a major adjustment. If you feel uncertain about how to incorporate the adjustment, you can ask to rehearse once before you tape, particularly if the scene is short. If the auditions are behind schedule, they may not be able to accommodate you. However, don't be afraid to ask. They may tape your rehearsal and give you the option of taping it again if you're not happy with it.

FLATTENING THE TEXT

When you first audition for the camera, you may think that anything you do will be too theatrical or too much, so you may have a tendency to "flatten" the text. Don't be frozen in space. Don't shut off your impulses and censor all your natural feelings and responses, throwing the baby away with the bathwater. Here, less is not more but less. So how can you avoid this trap? How do you know how much to do?

PRACTICE

I would suggest, if you do not own a videocamera, beg, borrow, or buy one. More and more auditions these days are for film and television, and actors' careers suffer from lack of experience in front of the camera. The more you see yourself, the more objective you will be.

Learn film and television scenes and practice them in front of the camera. You can easily set the camera on a table if you don't have a tripod, and place your chair so that you are in a medium close-up. If you can rehearse your scenes on camera at home for an actual audition you are about to have, you will go into the audition feeling a lot more confident. Practice with a friend who can adjust the camera and read the other lines with you, and you can exchange the favor. Observe yourself carefully. Tiny adjustments can make a huge difference: how you begin the scene, a moment of stillness, a small gesture that expresses an emotional state, a change in focus, a change in timing, how you listen, a release of tension in your face, how you end the scene, etc.

It's helpful to observe the camera technique of experienced, talented actors. When you watch movies or television, focus on a good actor in a medium close-up so you can get an idea of how he conveys thoughts and behavior within that frame.

NETWORK AUDITIONS

If you are being considered for a part as a regular in a network television series, all casting decisions must be approved by the network, which, usually, is based in L.A. If there is serious interest in you on the part of the director and producer of the show, you will be flown in to meet the folks at the network (unless, of course, you live in L.A.). This can be a bit hairy. You may have to fly to the coast on a day's notice, go directly from the airport to the studio, wait in the reception room with others who are competing for the role, and then walk into a room with a bunch of network people, who may expect you to be loose and funny and charming. All in a day's work, if you're lucky.

COSTUME

Because in film and television your appearance is a major factor in casting, the director will want to get some idea of what you would look like in character, if and when you play the part. So your clothes should suggest your character more than they might for theater auditions. (This does not include a transforming makeup, period costume, etc.) The elements of class—upscale, working class—and specificity of character will determine the kind of clothes you wear and, for women, the kind of makeup. If the character or the scene is sexy, you might wear a blouse or shirt with an open neck so you can touch your skin. It will suggest intimacy and will help you as much as it will the auditors.

Don't let your clothes make so strong a statement that they take the focus away from your face. Avoid bold colors. Bright, flowing scarves around your neck, bright ties with obtrusive prints, etc., are not a good idea. Solid colors are better than prints. The camera sometimes makes small or dense patterns vibrate. Avoid stripes. Light tends to bounce off stark white, though off-white is okay. Blue is good (especially if you have blue eyes). Avoid colors that might blend in with the color of your skin. You know what color you look best in. Avoid dangling earrings. Use your judgment and common sense.

SCRIPT

Scripts for film and television are written in a visual way. The action is sometimes described in extensive stage directions, almost as though the playwright is writing a novel. The stage directions give you clues as to the character, the "world of the play," the tone of the piece, and the acting atmosphere. Here's a stage direction from a television movie:

Bobby doesn't like this guy. He doesn't like cops in general. And this guy is definitely a cop. Cindy feels Bobby tensing, his heart pounding right through his fingertips. She rubs his arm. He ignores her.

And a stage direction from a sitcom:

Lisa playfully grabs Joan's arm and quite literally drags her to a little dance area. Joan stands there self-consciously for a few beats, then, egged on by Lisa, starts to bob her head a bit. Then she starts to move a bit more. It's obvious that she hasn't danced in years, except, y'know, liturgically, but she's at least trying. She studies other dancers near her and tries to mimic their moves. Though she looks awkward as hell, she's having a blast.

And a stage direction from a film:

They stand there, the ten feet between them filled with an energy both can feel. Maggie's blood runs. His eyes are so intense. So kind. They touch her in a deep way. . . . The question is so simple, so full of empathy . . . she is surprised, unnerved . . . the world seems to have shrunk to just this hallway. . . .

Get the picture? Since the dialogue tells you less in a film script than in a play, the stage directions may suggest images, moments, etc., that can help you make acting choices.

MISCELLANY

Sometimes a director at a camera audition will say, "Don't act." What she really means is, "Don't let me know you're acting." It doesn't mean that you must surrender your acting choices. It means you're being too obvious or theatrical and need to make an adjustment to the intimate and low-key requirements of camera work.

Keep your hair out of your face. If you don't, it will not only prevent the auditors from seeing you, you will have to keep pushing it away, distracting the auditors' focus from your work.

The way you sit is important. A slight slump or erect posture reflects an acting choice. Crossing your legs or not should also be an acting choice, as the camera reflects the posture of your entire body, even the part it doesn't show.

Television and film speech can be like a foreign language—idiomatic and full of jargon, especially in scripts about lawyers, doctors, or cops.

"Larceny by extortion? To make out a case for extortion, you have to plead value with specificity."

"DCG was called, the judge ordered an ex parte OTC, defendant was willing to nolo to allegations of neglect, and the child was placed into EFC."

"Yes, they found an infiltrating tubulo-lobular carcinoma, 1.5cm, estrogen positive, all twenty-six lymph nodes negative."

"Brass is breaking shoes we didn't grab the second shooter yet."

"We zeroed on a door-to-door. Cops swept the drug corners grabbing skels up looking for ways to associates of the D.O.A. perp."

"Angel can probably get us a short if we promise him some dynamite scag."

You need to rehearse the difficult phrases many times to make them sound like everyday speech and roll trippingly off your tongue. I remember auditioning for the role of a scientist in a sci-fi pilot. I had the line "I first noticed anomalies in the karotyping on their chromosome smears." I worked hard to make it sound natural and not trip over the words at the audition. It was perfect! But then I stumbled over the next sentence, "I need help analyzing the data." The tension had to go somewhere. Watch out!

If (a) the plot points seem very complicated, (b) you haven't read the whole script, and (c) you can't get help, you still have to act like you know what you're talking about.

ARE YOU WILLING TO BE PHOTOGRAPHED?

Some actors feel that the camera only reflects their physical shortcomings. Your nose is too big, too small, too crooked. Everybody can tell it's a nose job. Your eyes are too deeply set, your lips too thin. Your right profile is awful. And so forth.

If you don't look the way you would like to look, you may hide from the camera without realizing it. You try to obscure your physical "defects." You freeze your face for fear of expressing an idea or emotion that will make you look unattractive. You don't smile, or you play the scene largely in profile. In that way, you inhibit yourself; you don't commit fully to your acting choices; your focus is split between being in the moment and correcting your face.

When we look at ourselves on film or videotape, we don't always appreciate the wholeness or gestalt of who we are. Instead, we criticize what we think of as our imperfections. But when the auditors look at you, they don't focus on your nose or your ears, they respond to what Michael Chekhov calls your "individual atmosphere." Accepting and appreciating who you are and what you look like will reduce your self-consciousness, and it will help the auditors recognize and appreciate you.

We all know many successful actors in film and on television who do not have perfect faces, who are not conventionally gorgeous or handsome. We have strong feelings about these actors because we admire their work. Their faces are expressive, individual, and compelling to watch. It wasn't their physical beauty that brought them success; it was talent, hard work, and a belief in themselves.

MANNERISMS

If you have certain mannerisms, leave them at home when you audition for the camera. If you habitually blink a lot, bite your lip, flare your nostrils, keep your mouth open when you're not talking, clench your jaw, raise your eyebrows, or open your eyes too wide with each line, it won't help you get the part. Practicing in front of a camera at home is a good way to reduce or eliminate these mannerisms. Invite an actor friend who can be more objective about your mannerisms than you can to watch you on video. You *can* learn to act without them.

THE CAMERA AS A DOUBLE AGENT

Do you freak out in front of the camera? Do you feel that the camera is an enemy rather than an ally? Remember: the camera is working for *you* as well as for the director and producer. If you only ascribe the spy role to it, and are always tense and self-conscious in front of it, you can't take advantage of its power to enhance your performance.

If you do feel self-conscious in front of the camera, think of it as an object that you can endow with any qualities you choose. You can connect with the size, shape, color, or texture of the camera. Does it remind you of an object with which you have positive associations? A black jewel box, a rectangular journal, a camera of your own? Try transforming the lens of the camera into an eye you love, someone with whom you feel comfortable revealing yourself. You need to think about these connections and transformations before your audition, so that when you walk into the room, the camera will already be your friend, helping you land the job. *Acting in front of the camera is a partnership between you and the camera.*

We have all heard the expression, "The camera loves her." If you turn it around, and love the camera, you can get creative energy from its power of revelation.

Chapter VI

—■—

AUDITIONING FOR

MUSICALS

When Hal Prince asked me to cast musicals for him, I reminded him that I wasn't much of a singer or musician. Apart from a Welsh folk song in *Becket*, and "Matchmaker" in *Fiddler on the Roof*, I had never sung on the stage. Not to worry. I would work with a musical director who would evaluate voices, I would find the performers to audition and would evaluate their acting ability. Together, we would decide on the best candidates for the various roles in the show.

Fortunately, Paul Gemignani, a brilliant musical director, was my casting partner on most of Hal's shows, including *Follies, A Little Night Music, Pacific Overtures, On the Twentieth Century, Candide, Sweeney Todd, Evita, Merrily We Roll Along,* and *A Doll's Life*. We screened all the candidates and then decided who we would bring back to audition for Hal and the composer, producer, etc. What made our collaboration work was our mutual respect for the importance of both the singing and acting requirements of musical theater.

Paul was always willing to take the time to work with a performer whose voice was questionable if I was excited about her "rightness" for the role and her acting ability. Paul might change the vocal range of the song to see if the performer's voice sounded better in a higher or lower range. He might take her through arpeggios up and down the scales. Often, Paul would ask women to sing "Over the Rainbow" or "Summertime," songs that almost everybody seemed to be able to stumble through and that told him what he needed to know about their voices. He would ask men to sing "A New Town," "Fanny," or "Over the Rainbow." And lo and behold, sometimes we would discover that a performer could handle the songs in the show we were casting well enough, even though the initial presentation made it seem unlikely.

Likewise, if Paul was excited about a performer's voice and I thought his acting at the audition was hopeless, I would coach him in the scene and, if warranted, work with him privately after the initial audition. Sometimes we pulled it off.

GENERAL ADVICE

Here is some advice I received from Paul and others, and from my years of observing musical auditions.

Musical performers sometimes sabotage themselves at auditions by choosing songs that are too difficult for them. (Unless you've been asked to sing a song from the show you're audition-ing for, you choose your own material.) The performer may be able to sing the song at a voice lesson on a good day after thirty minutes of vocal exercises. But given the hazardous circum-stances of auditioning—for example, a long waiting time, an unknown accompanist, and often, nerves, which surely affect the ability to control breathing, chances are the performer may not be able to hit the tough notes every time. A performer sometimes attempts a difficult song, even though it is not the best choice for his voice, because he thinks he'll get extra points for choosing it. He won't, unless he sings it well. Deter-mine what may happen to you when you're under the gun, and make your choice of song accordingly.

If you have a break in your voice, work on the break with your voice teacher and hopefully you will smooth it out. But, for goodness sake, don't perform songs that reveal a break. (You'd be surprised at how many singers make this mistake!)

Sometimes a performer will sing something totally inconsis-tent with his/her image, e.g., a young, effete man singing a song of Jean Valjean's from *Les Mis,* an ingenue singing "The Ladies Who Lunch" from *Company,* or an elderly woman singing "Much More" from *The Fantasticks.* Be sure the songs you choose are more or less consistent with your age and the way you may be cast. There are many songs that are not defined by the age or type of the character who sings them and are fine for almost anyone to sing. Choose songs that you like and feel com-fortable singing from both a vocal and character point of view.

For the role of Phyllis in *Follies,* played by Alexis Smith, we needed a performer who could sing "Leave You," a song with lots of words sung very quickly. Paul said the only thing that saves you in a song like that is proper breath control and superb diction. If you don't breathe, we lose the lyric. If you don't articulate, we lose the lyric. If we lose the lyric, you lose the job!

Here are some critical notes from Paul's audition sheets over the years: Poor pitch, doesn't breathe, upper register wobbly, flat, sharp, scoops notes, too pop, no support, untrained, wrong notes, wide vibrato, "s" problem, pushed, voice too light, too operatic, croony, covered in upper register, voice won't mix, diction, nasal, out of tune, not yet—needs experience, one color, voice all over the place, recording voice.

Most of these comments are germane, no matter what the show. But taken together, Paul's notes identify pitfalls of which all musical auditioners should beware.

Paul is emphatic about not learning a song from a recording. Learn it from the sheet music so you don't end up with someone else's interpretation.

Don't sing a cappella. The producer will provide a piano and an accompanist. Bring your sheet music!

Don't choose long songs. Or if you do, cut the song to no more than thirty-two bars. If you sat with the auditors through eight hours of auditions in a day, you would appreciate the reason for this advice. At a general audition for a chorus role, you may be allowed to sing no more than sixteen bars, so choose your very best sixteen. Musical directors can tell after hearing only a few bars if they want to take you to the next step in exploring your voice, or want to call you back. The remainder of the time is spent evaluating range, acting ability, physical ease, etc. The auditors don't need a five-minute song to do that.

Paul suggests that women with both a head voice and a chest voice mention this at their first audition for a show. Usually you are asked to sing either in your head or your chest for a particular role. At a general audition, you will probably be asked to sing in both voices, if you have them.

For the musicals that Paul and I cast, which usually required a "legit" (trained) voice, he felt that revue material was not a good choice. (Revue material is any song that is not from a show or movie. It is generally a popular song, or may be special material written for a club act.)

Learn as much about a project as you can before you audition: the vocal range, the character you are auditioning for, what the musical is about, the other shows the composer and lyricist have written, etc. Paul feels the kiss of death is walking into an audition and saying, "What are you looking for?"

If you are called back, sing the same songs you did at the preliminary. Of course, if they ask you to sing something else or to learn a song from the score of the show for which you're auditioning, that's another story.

Some male singers enter an audition space and plant themselves stolidly with their legs quite far apart. We call it "the baritone stance." Their bodies are stiff and their gestures are wooden. If this sounds like something you do, try to stand and move more naturally without losing the fullness in your voice. Your singing teacher or coach can watch you while you sing and help to correct your stiffness.

Hal Prince says, "Don't stylize the song. Don't take liberties with the cadences. Be honest, intelligent, and simple. And watch your diction, especially the consonants." (He uses Mary Martin in *Peter Pan* and *South Pacific* as a role model for diction; mostly her t's and d's.)

Regarding the oft-asked question of whether you should sing a song written by a composer who may be present at the audition, Steve Sondheim says, "a composer has a very specific inner view of a song he/she's written, so if I were auditioning for a part, I'd steer clear of the work of anybody connected with the show."

Don't sing your song directly to the auditors. They will feel obliged to pay attention as though they were a member of the audience. Frequently, the auditors will need to consult with one another while you're singing. They don't feel comfortable doing that if you are looking directly at them. Imagine you are singing to someone over and in back of the heads of the auditors. If the song requires that you sing to the audience and it would be unnatural to visually skip over the auditors, include them but don't focus on them.

Arnold Mungioli, casting director, says, "Always be ready for anything. When casting *Ragtime,* we would audition for the role of Emma Goldman, who sings in the low-alto-belt range. Occasionally, a woman auditioning for Emma would be very right for one of the ensemble roles that understudied the role of

Emma Goldman. The understudy also needed to sing high soprano in the ensemble. We would ask if she sang soprano, and if so, request a soprano song. Some actresses were delighted, and charmingly accommodated our unexpected request. Other women argued that that was not what they were asked to prepare for the audition and go on about how they had not warmed up that part of their voice. Which, would you suppose were the women who got the job?"

When asked whether performing in a cabaret categorizes you as a cabaret performer, Marin Mazzie, who started out as a young performer in cabaret, says she feels it is valuable to work in the intimate setting of a cabaret, where you are face-to-face with the audience. As a leading performer in many Broadway musicals, it certainly didn't ruin her career.

PROTECT YOUR VOICE

Carolann Page is a superbly trained singer/actor and has some valuable advice for performers in the muscial theatre today: "The demands of today's musical-theater repertoire can take its toll on any voice. As actors/singers, we are expected to perform every musical style imaginable, from the lush lyricism of *Show Boat* and *Ragtime* to the pop/rock angularity of *Grease* and *Rent*. Add the 'Is it spoken or is it sung?' question constantly at play in Sondheim and we really have our hands full! It is therefore essential to continue voice lessons on a regular basis to solidify a technique that will enable the voice to handle eight shows a week. A vocal coach deals with style and phrasing, but the work with a voice teacher is essential in finding the correct vocal placement and position; securing the breath; and developing the confidence that enables a performer to handle nerves and avoid 'adrenaline' singing. A dancer would never think of going a week without class; an actor/singer must learn that same discipline . . . always remembering that singing is an athletic event!"

ACCOMPANIST

An accompanist is a bit like a reader. Unless you bring your own, you probably will be singing with the accompanist for the first time. Most accompanists are more reliable than most readers. Unlike readers, who frequently can't act, accompanists at least know how to read music and play the piano. They are trying to give you the musical support you need. They are on your side. However, if you have a big problem with the accompaniment, stop and start again. Treat the accompanist with respect. (He might be the musical director of the show or have worked for the producer for many years. Or he might be a relative of the director. You never know.)

Here is some advice from Paul Ford, Mandy Patinkin's accompanist and one of the best in New York. (He knows almost every song that was ever written and can transpose in a heartbeat.) Before you begin the audition, give the accompanist instructions in a calm fashion. Your instructions should include tempo, the number of verses, the retards, and chord symbols if it's transposed. The instructions should be planned in advance so you can give them explicitly and quickly. If the tempo needs to change, either stop singing or indicate the new tempo with a gesture.

If you bring your own accompanist, introduce him before you announce what you're going to sing. If not, be sure to thank the accompanist the producer provided when you pick up your music at the end of the audition. And if your audition doesn't go well, don't blame the piano player.

MUSICAL INTERLUDES

I've noticed that auditioning performers are often uncomfortable when there is a musical (nonvocal) interlude in the middle of the song. They move from one foot to the other. They don't know what to do with their hands. They drop out till it's time to sing again. Listen to the music. Stay in character. Prepare for the next vocal phrase, including any shift in the emotional quality of the song. Let the music help you make the transition. And breathe!

CHOREOGRAPHY

Feel free to respond to the music or the feeling of the song with gestures or movements. But gestures should be intuitive and natural, not stagey. No one expects you to choreograph the song. If you are singing a ballad, stand still and sing simply and truthfully. *If you are truly inhabiting the song, you can rarely do too little physically.* The auditors are evaluating your voice, not looking for your ability to dance while you sing. The choreographer will do that if you are called back and the show requires it.

ACTING THE SONG

Acting and singing are inseparable. Integration of the two is the key to dynamic musical auditioning, which applies as well, of course, to musical performing.

The good news is that you have a built in subtext—the music. The music often both supplies what the character feels and supports what he or she says. It serves to reinforce the lyric. For example, in "The Street Where You Live" (*My Fair Lady*), the music supplies Freddy, the character who sings it, with the romantic feeling that fully expresses how he feels about Eliza. Look for all the ways that the music helps carry and support your acting choices.

The music can also express what you are feeling and thinking but not always saying. For example, the music to "I'm Calm," from *A Funny Thing Happened on the Way to the Forum,* reflects Hysterium's nervousness. But the lyric is about how calm he is.

You can apply actable choices to your song. Not all actable-choices questions will be applicable to every song, but use them as a way of opening up your imagination to all the possible choices.

Listen to the music first. Then work on the text of the song, applying actable choices as needed. (It is helpful to think of the lyrics as a monologue.) Then learn the music and the lyrics together. If you learn the music before you know what the song is about, it is like learning your lines by rote before you've delved into their meaning. It's harder to change interpretation at that point.

Let's examine actable choices from a musical perspective:

1. Intuitive response:

The feeling of the whole, music and lyrics, will help you shape the song. Lyrics are usually full of images, which are a great resource in singing. If the images are not specified in the lyric, the idea of the lyric will help you find your own images. *When you connect an image with a musical phrase, it feeds and enriches your voice. It helps inspire the colors in your sound.*

Eliza Doolittle is the inspiration for the song "The Street Where You Live." But the images in the song are not of Eliza. So the performer would do well to imagine something about her: her face, something she wears, her smell, her walk, whatever provides an immediate sensory connection that elicits "the overpowering feeling" when she "suddenly appears."

2. The world of the song:

What is the style of the song? What is the context of the song? If it's from a show, read the script and check the other songs in the score to get a feel for the show. The world of *Phantom of*

the *Opera* is very different than that of *Crazy for You* or *1776* or
Cats. Think of how you would perform Ado Annie (*Oklahoma*),
Desirée (*A Little Night Music*), or Julie Jordan (*Carousel*).
What are the differences in the ways you would stand, gesture,
sing, and speak? Think of the physical aspects of your character: Sweeney (*Sweeney Todd: The Demon Barber of Fleet
Street*), Og (*Finian's Rainbow*), and Henry Higgins (*My Fair
Lady*) are strikingly different physical presences. *The world of
the song will be implicit in the way you sing and the way you
stand or gesture.* Just because you are using your voice beautifully, doesn't mean you can forget about your body. Your physicality will help in the presentation of the song because you will
be singing as the character. *Even if you don't move, it will help
you psychologically to know the physical nature of the character.*
You may choose to sing songs as yourself, not as the character
for whom the song was written, but it should be a conscious
decision.

3. What is the song about?

Is there a story? Does the song end differently than it began?
Think of the song as a one-act play. Be sure to read the verse in
the first part of the song, if there is one, even if you don't sing it
at the audition. It may set up the event of the song and give
you "the moment before." The song may have several inter-
ludes or bridges that move the story along and change the way
you sing each chorus. *Even if you only sing a portion of the song
for an audition, you need to know the whole story.*

4. Who is the character?

How can you evoke him or her? Sally Durant in *Follies* is romantic, unsophisticated, and repressed. In the song, "In Buddy's Eyes," she tells Ben, her old beau, that she has a happy life with her husband, Buddy, which we soon discover is not the case. She is still in love with Ben. Her romantic, unsophisticated, repressed qualities are apparent, but naming them as similarities or differences will reinforce your connection with who she is. Her later song "Losing My Mind," reflects her romantic yearning in a darker and more desperate way.

Billy Bigelow in *Carousel* characterizes himself as a "bum." He is self-destructive and reckless. But he has a loving, caring, optimistic side that creates a dynamic contrast with his wild and abusive side. *Finding polarities or contrasts will supply you with undertones that color the songs in a compelling way.*

If the character has very strong personal qualities, the character element may be the most actable choice in defining a song. Think of how these characters impact everything they sing: Jud (*Oklahoma!*), Rizzo (*Grease*), Joanne (*Company*), Engineer (*Miss Saigon*), Lucy (*You're a Good Man, Charlie Brown*), Carl Magnus (*A Little Night Music*), Angel (*Rent*).

5. What is your objective?

Why are you singing this song? What do you want to do? Often, when the singer is alone onstage, the song is an interior monologue, and the character's secrets are stated in the lyrics. In these cases, take the character at her word. However, it might trigger a more active response if you raise the stakes or find more active verbs.

In "Much More" (*The Fantasticks*), sung by Luisa, the whole song is based on "I'd like to . . . ," so the driving force is written into the lyric "I want much more than keeping house. . . ." The need is clear, but raising the stakes to "to break out" gives the need a physical image that may supply the singer with some extra oomph, particularly if she uses it as a pre-beat. The music switches from one vocal range to another; the song starts in soprano and goes to a chest voice, and back to soprano. The change in range illuminates the character's secret fantasies, giving the singer the musical support to deliver the emotional wallop of the song. *A change in vocal range often helps define a character's emotional state of being.*

In "Just You Wait," (*My Fair Lady*), Eliza's objective is to punish, torture, or kill Henry Higgins. The lyrics describe various fantasies in which she accomplishes one or the other of these objectives. (Those stakes are already about as high as you can get.) Before the song starts, Higgins says, "Eliza, I promise you you will pronounce your vowels correctly before this day is out, or there'll be no lunch, no dinner, and no chocolates!" The stage direction says, "Eliza, in a blind rage, slams her study book down on the floor and stamps on it." The intro is only a few chords, and you, Eliza, need to be in a rage. If you use the action described in the stage direction as an inner gesture, experiencing it in your imagination (perhaps imagining you are punching Higgins or twisting his head off may give you more energy!), the desire will be in your body and you'll be fired up when you begin to sing. The objective gathers momentum in the course of the song as Eliza allows her imagination to run wild. ("Just You Wait" was Julie Andrews's favorite song in *My Fair Lady*, by the way.)

In "A Little Priest" (*Sweeney Todd*), Mrs. Lovett wants to convince Sweeney to murder the men who come to his barber shop and then make meat pies out of them. A more active objective than "to convince him" might be "to inspire him" or "to manipulate him" or "to tantalize him." The *way* in which she accomplishes her objective is in the dotty and playful style of the character, suggested and supported by the music and lyrics.

In "I Cain't Say No" (*Oklahoma!*), Ado Annie is an honest, down-to-earth, rough-and-tumble character who loves to flirt, kiss, and fool around with guys. She tells us she knows it's not moral but men sweep her off her feet and she loses control because "she cain't be what she ain't." Here's my take on the song. Annie seems to be asking for our understanding and for us to forgive her for being who she is. She tells us she weakens and loses control when she's having a good time. But don't be misled. She's not in "a turrible fix." Who she is and what she wants becomes apparent in the lyrics of the song and in the lively, playful tempo of the music. She clearly wants to continue "to flirt, kiss, and fool around with guys!" No point in overcomplicating a simple idea. She has no secrets. She's telling all. *The character's objectives can only be divined by taking into account the whole lyric, the tempo of the song, and the character as expressed by the combination of both.*

Some songs may not have an easily accessible objective. Don't sweat over it. Look for a different actable choice that is a defining element in the song.

6. What is your obstacle?

What's in your way? In Ado Annie's case, it's the fact that, while she knows what's right and wrong, "when I'm with a feller, I fergit!" Morality is her obstacle, though given how much she enjoys herself, I'd say it was a losing battle from the start. Her attitude toward the obstacle gives the song a joyfulness; underneath she knows she will win and achieve her objective—to flirt, kiss, and fool around with guys—against all obstacles!

In the case of Mrs. Lovett, her obstacle is Sweeney's possible reaction to what she is inspiring him to do—to commit heinous crimes. To defuse the obstacle, she has to color her actions so that they appear delicious, exciting, and fun rather than dangerous and immoral.

Billy Bigelow's obstacle is the part of himself that is self-destructive and reckless. It makes the sweetness of his wanting "to father" even sweeter; it is so far from his past behavior and how he thinks of himself.

7. What are the relationships?

Who are you singing to? What is your relationship to the person you are singing to or about? Is this person real or imagined? How do you feel about her? Is she facing you or turned away? Are you singing to yourself? Are you singing to the audience?

Tevye sings "If I Were a Rich Man" (*Fiddler on the Roof*) to himself, but the song relates to all the people in his life: his wife, his daughters, the rabbi, the congregation. If you are auditioning for Tevye, you want to imagine what all these characters look like and how you feel about them, so they come to life every time you sing the song. You also need to think about how you relate to God, to whom Tevye speaks in the song. (*When auditioning, try to place most of your images somewhere on the fourth wall, so we can see your face.*)

When Billy Bigelow sings "Soliloquy" (*Carousel*), he relates to his imagined, wished-for son or daughter in very specific ways, as though they were in front of his eyes. His excitement at being a prospective father overflows; he is lost in his fantasies. If you are singing the role, find images of children who inspire you, either from your own life or made up from your imagination, so you can deliver those lyrics as fully as they deserve.

8. *Where are the moments?*

They usually happen where the composer and lyricist have written them into the music and lyrics. You have to decide which ones are the most dynamic, and supply them with the power of your acting choice. Steve Sondheim talks about how Oscar Hammerstein taught him the value of such moments: the "power of a single word and the ability of music to get that word to explode."

One example in Sondheim's own work is in "Losing My Mind" (*Follies*) when Sally sings, "You said you loved me, or were you just being k-i-n-d?" the second time in the song. The word "kind" on the higher note is a thrilling moment in the song and reflects the depth and intensity of her fears.

When Billy Bigelow calls his son by the name Bill for the first time, the composer has provided a pause for Billy when he realizes he has named him for himself. It is a cappella, and is a beautiful and defining moment. Another is when he realizes his wife, Julie, might have a girl. When he sings, "You have to be a father to a girl," the tone of his voice must soften and caress the lyric. The music and lyric support you emotionally, but you need to be aware of the moment to take full advantage of what you are given.

9. What is the atmosphere?

In Jonathan Tunick's introduction to the printed version of *A Little Night Music*, he says, "During the course of the preliminary discussions of *A Little Night Music*, Stephen Sondheim remarked that he imagined 'the atmosphere to be perfumed— of musk in the air.' My immediate reply was 'plenty of strings.'" The music provides you with the atmosphere or landscape of the song.

There are times when the atmosphere of the song changes, only to subsequently raise the stakes when the song goes back to the original atmosphere. For example, Eliza in "Just You Wait" begins in a warlike atmosphere. Then the tempo and the style of the music provide a transition to a tone of sweetness and gaiety when she fantasizes about the king proclaiming Eliza Doolittle Day. The warlike atmosphere is then taken to a new high when she fantasizes that Higgins is led to the firing squad and she commands the troops to fire on him.

10. What is the pre-beat?

Check what happens in the scene just before the character sings. It might lead you to your pre-beat. Use any of the pre-beats suggested earlier: objective, inner gesture, obstacle, atmosphere, relationship, costume, image, "the cry," or anything else that occurs to you that will help you prepare to enter the song. Take the three or four seconds to tap into the pre-beat, and give the accompanist a nod when you're ready for him to begin. You will be helped mightily by the musical intro the accompanist plays. Listen to it. Use it to breathe in whatever you need to tap into the pre-beat, and be present, vocally and otherwise, on your first note.

ACTING THE MUSICAL SCENE

Use actable choices to mine the text as you would in any play. Musical scenes are often shorter and more compact than in nonmusicals. That doesn't mean the character's thinking or emotional life is necessarily simple and uncomplicated. You want to audition the scenes with an understanding of the character, the event, the objectives, the relationships, etc.

Music brings an energy into the theater that is unique to the musical-theater form. The music of the overture, the songs, the dance music, the music scored under the dialogue, all create a theatrical energy that becomes a defining element for the actor who performs in the musical theater. You may not have heard the score if it is a new musical, but you must pay attention to that heightened energy when you are preparing your audition.

Chapter VII

—————

MONOLOGUES

In addition to auditioning for specific roles in plays, movies, or television, actors who are not yet well established in the profession are sometimes called upon to do so-called general auditions.

A general audition is designed to reveal the actor's quality, talent, and range rather than his suitability for a particular part. General auditions are held by theater schools and conservatories to select the students they will admit; by agents to find new and undiscovered talent; and by casting directors and regional theaters to add to the pool of talent they call upon when casting new projects. From an actor's point of view, the general audition can be a very valuable tool in advancing his career. Seize the opportunity!

Typically, what happens at a general audition is that the

actor performs two contrasting monologues of his own choosing. A monologue may be a soliloquy in which the character speaks to himself, or it may be a speech taken from a scene in which the character addresses another character at length and without interruption, although the other character is not physically present and must be imagined by the actor. The contrast may be provided by choosing one monologue that is comedic and another that is dramatic, or one that is classical and another that is contemporary.

Usually, you are given a total of four or five minutes to perform two monologues. You will know well in advance of the audition how much time you have and what your options are.

The auditors at a general audition understand the difficulty faced by the actor in performing a monologue. It is an inherently unnatural theatrical form in which the actor must work alone. If it is a soliloquy, it is out of context, and if it is taken from a scene with another character, you don't even have a reader on the stage to help you. (That could be a blessing!) *However, the auditors expect more of a finished performance than they expect at an audition for a specific role.* They assume you have selected the monologue to reveal your own special talent. You may have unlimited time to prepare. And you have the liberty of staging the piece as you see fit.

Here are some suggestions as to how to choose, prepare and perform monologues for general auditions.

CHOOSING A MONOLOGUE

Casting director Daniel Swee says, "It's helpful to cast yourself well when you pick a monologue. It's the equivalent of giving someone a clear snapshot of you, because it's often their first time meeting you. Maybe later on, they can see the whole range of what you can do."

1. Well in advance of scheduling any particular general audition, you should choose a number of contrasting monologues for use at general auditions and have them fully prepared, memorized, and readily available to you. This will save time, anxiety, and pressure in preparing for any particular general audition and allow you to focus on selecting the monologues best suited for the occasion. It will give you time to refresh and refine your performance. Your repertoire of monologues should include at least two classical pieces, one comedic and one dramatic (one should be in verse), a contemporary comedy, and a contemporary drama. If you have chosen monologues that seem too big for a small space, choose a couple of additional ones that will work in an office, which is where some agents and casting directors may ask you to perform.

2. Choose your monologues carefully. Good monologues are hard to find. Don't settle for the mediocre. Keep looking until you find monologues that you can connect with, that you can inhabit rather than just represent, monologues that you love

and can continue to use over a long period of time. Janet Zarish, head of acting in New York University's Graduate Acting Department, says about actors auditioning for the program, "We see the same monologue over and over, but we'll listen and are thoroughly engaged if it's true in thought and unique to who you are, if it's spoken through your own individual understanding."

Although monologues are usually taken from plays, they may be found in film or television scripts as well. You may be able to piece together a monologue from a character's dialogue in a scene with another character. Monologues can be taken from novels. An actor with a literary flair can write his own monologue. There are many books of monologues, but the best pieces are overused.

A good monologue is like a one-act play, with a beginning, middle, and end. It should be well written; it should develop, and take you on a journey where something happens to you. It should not be cluttered with too many references, either to the plot or to the names of other characters; such references may prove confusing to your auditors if they are unfamiliar with the source. A good monologue engages the auditors from the get-go and compels them to listen. (If the monologue engages *you*, it will probably engage the auditors.)

3. Monologues should be no longer than two minutes. If you are given five minutes to do two monologues, choose two two-minute monologues and use the extra minute for your pre-

beat and for making the transition from one monologue to the other. The auditors need that moment in between to make the transition as well. (Turning upstage helps to make that transition.) If you move too quickly from one monologue to the other, your acting will appear mechanical. And you will surely improve your performance if you feel you don't have to rush through the audition. Another reason for not using up all of your allotted time in performing: if you exceed it, your auditors may cut you off. Because audition sessions keep to a tight schedule, they often use a stopwatch.

4. Choose a monologue that is more or less age appropriate. Stay away from characters much older or much younger than you are. You want your auditors to find you believable. You want to make it easy for them to imagine how you might be cast in upcoming projects. A young actor may stretch his talent and his range by playing King Lear in an acting class; but, for a general audition you want to put your best foot forward and be as accomplished and authentic as possible.

5. Beware of monologues that are narrative in form. They may tell an interesting story, but may not allow you to make acting choices that arise from strong needs or desires that will reveal your acting ability.

6. Beware of monologues that, taken out of context and performed on their own, become melodramatic. Medea may be a role

you perform brilliantly, but two minutes of Medea, coming out of the blue, may be too difficult for you to perform and for your auditors to watch. A monologue doesn't have to have fireworks to be impressive. Quiet pieces with emotional subtleties are appreciated and often reveal an important dimension of the actor's talent.

7. Beware of monologues that are too familiar. If you can perform Hamlet's "To be or not to be" with clarity, understanding, depth of feeling, a particular point of view, and excellent vocal and language skills, go for it. But unless you are confident you have the chops to do that, you are better off choosing less familiar material.

PREPARATION

8. In preparing your monologue, use the actable choices, which should be as helpful in preparing a monologue as in preparing to audition for a specific role.

9. In preparing to perform the monologue, get some professional coaching if you can afford it. Or have someone you trust give you some direction. You can always ignore direction or criticism if you choose, but intelligent direction or criticism may enhance your performance.

10. Make sure that, in preparing the monologue, you read not only the scene, but the entire play, film, television script,

or novel from which it is taken. Understanding the work as a whole can only give your performance more depth.

11. If you have created your own monologue by combining into a single speech several shorter speeches addressed to another character, and there are points at which you feel you must pause to imagine the response of the other character, you should not exceed one or two brief pauses. You will be better off if you make a small adjustment or rewrite that will eliminate the pauses altogether.

12. Everybody loves to laugh. So if you are only allowed one monologue at your general audition, and you can do it well, choose a comedic piece.

PERFORMING THE MONOLOGUE

13. If you are speaking to an imagined character in your monologue, you can imagine that character on the stage with you, more or less in the same position that a reader would be likely to occupy, to the side and downstage. If you wish, use a chair in place of your imagined character so that you will have a real object to focus on. (But beware. If you are standing and your imagined character is sitting in the chair, you may tend to look down too much.) You can place the character on the back wall, slightly off center, so that you are not looking, and do not appear to be looking, directly at your auditors. (This is the

most common practice.) If you choose, and if it makes sense in the scene, the imagined character can be moved around in your imagination during the course of the monologue.

14. Wherever you choose to place or move the imagined character, don't feel obliged to address the entire monologue directly to him. As I mentioned earlier, it is important to get in the habit of relating to other characters naturally. Find places where you can turn away. The majority of actors performing monologues addressed to other characters fall into the trap of directing all their lines to that character, which paralyzes them physically and undermines the believability of their acting.

15. If you are talking to an imagined audience rather than another character, don't talk directly to the auditors. Speak around the auditors and above their heads, letting your eyes fall on the auditors only now and then, as part of the audience. Looking directly at the auditors throughout the monologue may be somewhat unnerving for them and for you, and will diffuse your focus and concentration.

16. If you are talking to an imagined audience, decide what your relationship is to that audience. Are they good friends, parents, confidantes, strangers, lovers, enemies? When Paul Newman directed the film version of *The Glass Menagerie,* he told John Malkovich, who was playing Tom, to talk to the audience "as though we were a lady you were inviting into your head."

17. Actors have a tendency to rush through their monologues. Take the time you need to connect with your thoughts and images. Allow your thoughts to land. Don't fly over them.

18. At the end of your monologue, you may find yourself waiting for the auditors to say thank you. They may not be familiar with the material, or, even if they are, they may not realize your monologue has come to an end. Take a beat and say "Scene" to let them know you are done.

Melissa Smith, conservatory director at the American Conservatory Theater in San Francisco, says, "Choose audition pieces that you have a passion to speak. Then bring your *self* to the audition—and be *present* in the interview. I want to get a sense of the person in the work and the person I'll work *with* should you come to our school."

After Janet Zarish and Zelda Fichandler, chair of the Graduate Acting Program at New York University, returned from a trip where they auditioned eight hundred actors in many different cities for admission to the NYU program, Janet said, "The biggest mistakes were that the stakes were too casual, not costly enough, not important enough. They were slight needs; logical, true, but uninvested."

Zelda Fichandler says, "Come forward, compel us to admit you; send your spirit out."

Chapter VIII

———————

THE AUDITIONING EVENT:

A PRACTICAL GUIDE

Apart from mastering the technique of auditioning, you must learn to cope with the practical realities of the auditioning event. Here are some suggestions that may help.

PREPARATION

Usually your audition will be scheduled anywhere from a few days before the audition to one day in advance. If you squeeze in your preparation in the last hours before your audition, you will expect less of yourself and won't do your best. Sometimes you won't have enough advance notice to prepare fully and will have to make do. But if you get in the habit of preparing as much as possible before your audition, you will be more likely to find the time that is needed. If you must, cancel social engagements and other activities to get the preparation time you need. If you are serious about getting work in this profession, you have to take each audition seriously. Prepare!

PHYSICAL READINESS

It should be self-evident that you can't do your best at an audition if you don't have a sense of physical well-being. If you are tired and sluggish, or hung over, or, for whatever reason, unable to fully use your voice and body at the audition, you will compromise your chances. Yet many actors give short shrift to such considerations in preparing for an audition. Don't make that mistake. To reduce nervous tension and feel in control, it helps to feel in good physical condition. Eat and drink moderately the night before the audition, get enough sleep, and do some warm-up exercises for your voice and body before you go to the audition. If, for whatever reason, you are ill or not at your physical best, try to reschedule your audition. If you cannot reschedule, and you decide to go to the audition, have your agent call the casting director and tell her you're under the weather. *But don't apologize for your condition at the audition.*

SUPPORT SYSTEM

Some NYU Graduate Acting alumni formed a small auditioning-support group, made up of four actors/friends. If an actor in the group has an audition scheduled, he calls someone else in the group to help him prepare by reading the scene with him, and asks the other members of the group to critique his audition and offer suggestions. It's a good idea if you can arrange it. When preparing, have your friend/reader play the other character in the scene in a variety of different ways. Camryn Manheim, actor on the TV series *The Practice,* suggests that if you are auditioning for Romeo, you should have your friend/reader read Juliet like Lucille Ball, just so you will be prepared for any eventuality.

This may sound unrealistic and like overkill. How can you possibly devote so much time and attention to every audition? Of course, it's not possible to prepare fully for every audition. *However, when you take care of yourself and set the stage for your best work, you feel more confident going in.* If you get in the habit of incorporating best-possible preparation before your auditions, you will be more likely to find the time as a matter of course.

SCRIPT

If possible, try to read the whole script before the audition. It will illuminate far more about your character and your audition scene than reading only the scene by itself or "the sides," as they are called in the trade. Usually, the entire script of a new film, TV, or theater project is sent to agents. So, if you have an agent, and she has scheduled an audition for you, she should provide you with a copy. If you have an appointment for an audition but don't have an agent, or your agent doesn't have the full script, call the producer's office. Find out if the script is available. Maybe you can sit in the producer's reception room for an hour and read it. It's worth a try. You may even be able to get the script overnight. Anything you can do to help prepare more fully for your audition is worth trying. Actors are sometimes afraid to ask for the script if it is not offered. Don't be timid. No casting director, producer, or director is going to think less of you for going the extra mile to give a better audition.

If you can't get the entire script, the next best thing is to get your audition scene as soon as you can. If you don't have a fax or e-mail, perhaps you can have it faxed to a friend that lives nearby, or to your local copy shop. In any event, be resourceful.

In Los Angeles, some of the film studios where film and television auditions are often held are hard to find. So, if you haven't been there before, you might ask the casting director if you can pick up the script or sides at the studio casting office before the day of the audition. That way, you won't get lost on your way to the audition. As a New York actor in L.A., on my way to a studio audition, I have driven off the freeway at the wrong exit, stumbled around till I found my way, and not realized the amount of time I needed to park my car and walk what seemed like the twelve miles from the parking area to the casting office, which is usually hard to find. (All the buildings look alike.) And it always seems to be 110° in the shade. Needless to say, I was not in great shape when I arrived at my audition.

Suit yourself. Whatever you do, allow yourself plenty of time.

CAST BREAKDOWNS

A cast breakdown is a brief description of each of the characters in a play, movie, or television show. Cast breakdowns are prepared for and sent to agents so they can decide who among the actors they represent are suitable candidates for the various parts to be cast in New York City, cast breakdowns for plays, musicals, and film projects appear in *Backstage* and *Show Business,* two weekly trade papers. For L.A.-based productions, they appear in *Backstage West* and *Dramalogue.* Casting news is also available on the Web.

Cast breakdowns are sent out by Breakdown Services, a company that provides this service to agents. Sometimes, Breakdown Services prepares the breakdown; sometimes it is prepared by the casting director. Often the breakdown is taken from the author's character descriptions that appear in the script.

Get the character description from the cast breakdown as soon as you can. The description may give you some idea of how the author and/or the director see the character. Even if it doesn't tell you much—e.g., "She is a college student whose roommate stole her boyfriend" or "He is a Wall Street lawyer, 25–30"—when you are preparing an audition and have only a fragment or an inscrutable scene to work with, any information or guidance is helpful.

COLD READINGS

The term "cold reading" describes an audition at which the actor does not have the opportunity to read the whole script, or even the audition scenes, in advance. You will see the audition scene for the first time on the day of your audition when you arrive at the audition site.

Here are some suggestions as to how to deal with cold readings.

1. Try to find out when the audition session will begin, so you can get there as early as possible. If you have some time to work on the scene before you are scheduled to audition, instead of racing through it in five or ten minutes, you are apt to give a better audition.

2. Bring a highlighter (yellow is the best) to mark your lines. It will make the scene easier to read during the audition.

3. If the sides you are given include the end of the previous scene or the beginning of the next scene, check them for clues that might give you useful information.

4. Sometimes, when you have a short time to prepare, panic kicks in and your concentration is all over the place. Your internal monologue is, "I don't know what I'm doing! I am clueless!" Needless to say, that feeling is not conducive to

delivering a good, confident audition. You tend to skim the scene quickly and focus only on your character's lines. Fight the tendency. You are better off reading through the scene carefully, even if you have time to read it only once. That way, you will at least have an idea of what the whole scene is about.

5. Even if you have little time, see if you can find an actable choice or two that will give you a handle on the scene. *Keep your acting choices simple.* If you're too ambitious in a cold reading, you're apt to go way off the track. Trust your intuition.

6. Sometimes you will be asked to give a cold reading of a comedic scene in which the characters have a series of very short speeches. In a scene of this kind, you feel compelled to pick up every cue and keep up a performance rhythm, which is very difficult to do when you haven't had much preparation time. Try to relate to your partner and play the scene without sacrificing everything but the rhythm. This can be tricky because the humor is often dependent on the rhythm of the scene. Use your best judgment about how to maintain the comic timing without losing everything else.

7. If you're dyslexic or have some other reading problem, let the casting director know and ask for the script in advance of your audition. Don't be embarrassed. Reading problems are not uncommon among actors. Most casting directors will try to accommodate you.

8. Cold readings can work in your favor. They can be liberating. You don't have time to censor your intuitive responses or to overthink the material. Actors often like cold readings best because they don't feel as responsible for giving a "performance" as they would in a prepared reading or a callback.

9. On occasion, after an audition for which you were well prepared, the director may ask you to read a different scene, one you've never seen before. "Oh, just read it . . . ," she says. Don't imagine you will get extra points for reading it ice-cold. The extra points will come from giving a good reading. So ask for a few minutes outside the audition room to look it over. Chances are the director will agree. If you're still not ready when called to read, ask if someone else would like to go first. (Actors always have time problems.) Fight for the time you need. Being a good boy or girl and doing what you're told or what you think will please the auditors is not what auditioning is about. It's about the quality of your work.

MEMORIZING

The bottom line in evaluating your audition is not about whether you have memorized the material. It is about your acting and how well you fit the part. You must balance your preparation time, so the greater portion of it is on your acting. But, to the extent you can memorize the material, or at least become very familiar with it, you will be ahead of the game.

Because you are no longer tied to the script, you will feel much freer to play the scene and to protect the continuity of listening and responding. If you rely too heavily on the script, you are apt to miss transitions in the scene, which are often the most interesting acting moments. Even so, you should always have the script to refer to, like a security blanket, so your focus is not on remembering the lines. The script also can serve as a prop—then you have only one hand to worry about.

You may have memorized the script, more or less, and you can play the scene without looking at the script for pages at a time. But what happens if suddenly your memory fails and you try frantically to find the right page? As part of your preparation, memorize where to turn the page, so you will automatically be on the right page if and when you need to refer to the script.

If you have a line that is interrupted from one page to the next, write the continuation of the sentence at the bottom of the page, so if you can't remember the rest of the sentence you don't have to turn the page in the middle of the line.

You may feel you know the script cold. But when you are auditioning, the words fly out of your head. Don't struggle to remember. Refer to the script whenever you need to. Try not to ad lib.

In auditioning for the camera, it is more important to memorize the material. The camera needs to see your face, particularly your eyes and not the top of your head looking down at the script. (See chapter V, Auditioning for the Camera.)

Auditioning without a script in hand can have a psychological effect on the auditors, albeit a subtle one. They will expect a more finished performance. There is the rare audition at which you feel ready to give a performance and you don't want to hold the script, like Kevin Kline in his audition for *On the Twentieth Century* (see page 180). That's great if you feel ready to do so. But be absolutely sure you can fulfill the raised expectation of a full performance.

THE WAITING PERIOD

While you are waiting your turn to audition, you are apt to be in some kind of waiting room or reception area, or backstage in a theater. The space is probably unfamiliar. Generally, unfamiliar places can make you feel uncomfortable. That, combined with your natural apprehension about being judged, contribute to a feeling of alienation or discomfort. How can you warm up the space, make it your own, make it a creative space?

1. Think about a space where you feel at ease: your own room, an outdoor space you love, a rehearsal hall or stage you know well, a place you've thought about before and can summon up easily. Find something similar to your own more familiar "creative space" in the real space around you. It might be the color of the walls, the carpet or floor, the lamp, the desk, a plant, a telephone, or a window. You can always find some connection between the real and your own familiar space. An object doesn't have to be identical to the one in your familiar

space. "There's a table lamp on that desk. There is a table lamp in the room in my imagination." The lamp becomes a familiar object. *Making a palpable connection immediately alters your feeling of alienation and connects you with the sensation of your familiar place.* If there is absolutely nothing you can think of, you can use your concentration and imagination to change an object or element in the room to the desired one. In any event, put something in the room that you can relate to.

2. You can also look at the reception room as if you were your character, and ask yourself how your character would function in this environment. "How would she sit in this chair? Has my character ever been in an office in a city? Would she feel comfortable here?" You can do all of this without moving from your seat, or exhibiting any weird behavior.

3. You might put something into your purse or pocket that reminds you of the character. It might be an object that you have endowed with a special meaning. Just handling it, connecting with it, knowing it's there can ground you. I was once in Lanford Wilson's *The Great Nebula of Orion*. My character had a very complicated relationship with her mother, who had a passive-aggressive personality. Mark Zeller, my director, suggested I put insecticide inside a perfume bottle and leave it on the coffee table on the living room set. Everytime my eyes passed over it, my character's relationship with her mother became immediate and visceral. You don't have to do anything

this complicated for an audition, but objects can powerfully stimulate your senses.

4. Actors tend to read their lines over and over while waiting to audition. What is more productive, if you have had adequate time to prepare, is to read over the lines of the other character in the scene. It should help you enter the world of the play and give you a fresh attack on your own lines when you audition. Then you can focus on your pre-beat.

Any focus that gets you out of your "I'm so nervous" space into your creative space is helpful.

5. If you are auditioning in a theater, you will be waiting backstage. I think the theater atmosphere is an easier one in which to prepare, because unlike the reception room in an office, it feels like the real thing. It might be helpful to tune in to another backstage at a theater where you were performing when your creative juices were flowing and you were feeling confident about your work. You can think about those times and places in advance, so that anytime you audition in a theater, you can call up the physical sensations connected with them. You don't have to get lost in a specific role you've performed in the past, just before you audition, but you can surely use the energy and power connected with a positive experience of performing on the stage.

6. Always arrive early for the audition. You never know in advance what the conditions of the waiting space will be, so give yourself time to get acclimated, centered, and focused. Many actors arrive just in time to go into an audition and are not warmed up until they're ready to leave. Don't get caught unprepared.

7. You are responsible for auditioning at your appointed time. If you are asked to go in early, don't try to please the casting director by agreeing to audition before you're ready. (Remember, there are no gold stars or graham crackers awarded to good little actors.) Unless you are ready and don't want to wait, do the casting director a favor; wait until you are ready, give a good audition, and get the part.

As a casting director, I have been in the reverse situation. An actor missed his appointment, and the director and I were left sitting and twiddling our thumbs waiting for the next actor. I understand the casting director's frustration. However, if your audition is undermined by starting too soon, the casting director will have to spend a lot more time looking elsewhere to cast the role.

8. While you're waiting to audition, there is sometimes a social element that conspires against you. You may see friends you haven't seen for a long time who want to chat. That can be very appealing because it distracts you from your audition anx-

iety (if you have it). If you're an actor who wants to be distracted, you can skip to the next paragraph. But chatting may prevent you from focusing on what you are about to do. You can greet your friend and say, "I need to look at my script. Can I see you afterward?" If your friend can't wait for you, exchange telephone numbers. He or she will probably be grateful to you. Remember, everybody is in the same boat. Don't be embarrassed or think it uncool to want to prepare. I consider it very cool. Why be embarrassed to be an actor who takes auditioning seriously?

9. There may be other distracting elements in the waiting area. I remember waiting in a small reception room where a casting assistant was having a personal chat on the phone. She talked so loudly I found it almost impossible to concentrate on my audition. If something like that happens to you, fight to keep your focus on your work. However, if the only emotion you experience is anger, try to convert the energy from your anger and use it in your scene. Or go out in the hall or to the bathroom to preserve your audition focus. You can't expect reception rooms to be like Buddhist retreats, but it is, nonetheless, infuriating when the auditors or their staff are insensitive to the actors' needs.

10. Let's say you've been waiting an hour. You arrived full of beans, raring to go. But now you're tired, annoyed, impatient,

your energy is low. Usually you can check a list to see how many actors are scheduled to audition before you. When there are only one or two, start focusing on your energy sources in the scene. If there are too many people around to concentrate on your preparation, it's the hall or the bathroom again! (If there are people in the bathroom, go into a stall.) Focus on whatever will get you to where you want to be at the start of your audition. Whatever that may be, you should have rehearsed it in advance, so you can tap into it.

Fight for your actor's concentration. Don't sabotage your work by taking a laissez-faire attitude: "I'm fine. I know this cold. I can talk to friends. I don't need to prepare. I'm a pro." Maybe so, but why not get yourself together and feel centered and ready to go?

11. Sometimes a long waiting period is no one's fault. Perhaps the casting director wanted the director to see as many actors as possible and overbooked the session, assuming, as frequently happens, that some would drop out. If she hadn't overbooked, you might not have been called. If the casting director hasn't worked with the director before, she may not know the pace at which the director works. Also, if the director is interested in someone, he may want to spend some additional time with that actor. That actor could be YOU. So try not to let yourself get whipped into a frenzy and risk ruining your audition with the hostility you bring into the room. If

you're that angry, tell them you have another appointment and try to reschedule.

There are times when the folks running the audition seem irresponsible. A young actor friend of mine in L.A. recently had an appointment for a third callback on a film. Because his original audition had been taped, he thought it odd to be called back so many times without any explanation. He traveled an hour to get to the audition. He arrived for his 11:00 A.M. appointment on time and was told that a message had been left for him at his home at 10:45 A.M. that his appointment had been changed to "a little after 1:00 P.M." He swallowed hard and left for two hours. When he came back at 1:06 P.M., he was told the director had just gone out for lunch, and was asked to come back at 2:00 P.M. He was furious. He said, "No, thank you, I am not coming back. If you don't want to offer me the part based on a taped audition and two callbacks, that's okay. Good-bye." He did not get cast. In a similar situation, you have to decide whether to defuse your anger and extend yourself, or leave and perhaps lose the job. It's your call.

NERVES

Austin Pendleton, actor, director, writer, and teacher, says, "Don't deny your nerves. Acknowledge them. Then focus on the work."

Nobody can wave a magic wand and make your nerves disappear. But you can change the focus from your nerves to whatever focus you've chosen for your audition scene. If you've ever been in a noisy subway train while reading a book, you might remember looking up from your book and suddenly hearing the sound of the train. While you were reading, you didn't hear the train. You can't concentrate on two things at the same time. If you're concentrating on how nervous you are, you're not able to fully concentrate on the task at hand.

I remember a final audition for a Prince-Sondheim musical in a Broadway theater. A young actor started her audition by saying, "I'm so nervous!" There was a silence in the theater. How could we respond? "Don't be nervous, we're just folks?" or "We're nervous, too"? or "Do you want to come back another time?" She may not have realized it, but she was asking us not to expect too much of her and to give her a break. We tried to reassure her as best we could, but it was an awkward moment for everyone. Auditors know very well that most actors get nervous. But they expect them to be professional enough to control their nerves and not talk about it.

Ask yourself what it is about the audition that makes you so nervous. Try to address those issues. Are you afraid of appearing foolish for making strong choices that could be "wrong"? Are you feeling desperate about getting this particular job because you are running out of money? Are you putting a great deal of importance on this audition because you think it will change your life? That's a lot of stress. Analyze the problem, don't avoid it. That may help relieve the pressure, which can only hurt your audition.

Whether you get nervous or not, here's a breathing exercise that moves you into a good pre-audition place. It can be done in a crowd of people without anyone noticing. It takes the same amount of time it takes to breathe. If after reading this book you remember nothing but this breathing exercise, you will have learned something of value.

While you're waiting to go into the audition space, get in touch with your natural rhythm of breathing. Focus on your inhalation and your exhalation. As you inhale, breathe in a sensation of openness. Let the openness flow into your body, releasing some of your tension. Then, exhale a sensation of openness. Imagine you are opening the space around you with your exhalation, filling the room with openness. You are opening yourself inside and opening the space outside with your breath. With this exercise, you can create your own personal workspace, released from debilitating tension. You should be able to do this with only a few breaths. Since your adrenaline is flowing, it's hardly likely that you will space out or go into a meditative state. If you feel at all spacey, stop!

Most actors have "healthy nerves," nerves that give you a level of energy which can then be transformed and pumped into your acting. But some actors are affected noticeably by the pressure of auditions. Their hands shake, their knees get weak, they get red, they sweat, or sometimes their breath seems to stop. If you give yourself time to prepare, ground

yourself in actable choices, raise your auditioning consciousness, and use the breathing exercise I described, you will
enhance your ability to work under pressure and the worst
symptoms of nervousness should be reduced. However, if you
are severely afflicted, and your nerves are more than you can
handle, I would suggest you get professional help, or perhaps
consider another profession. Auditions will not go away.

ENTRANCE

A common myth about auditions is that the director decides
whether to hire you when you walk in the door. Not true! Yes,
an impression is certainly made when you first appear. Everything contributes to that impression: your clothes, your attitude, your energy, your social manner, etc. The director may be
thinking, "Oh, great! She looks like what I imagine the character might look like." (Hope springs eternal in casting sessions.)
Or he may be thinking, "She looks anxious, insecure, intimidated, or too eager to please. She might behave like that on
opening night."

You may be *feeling* anxious, insecure, intimidated, and eager
to please, but use your acting ability to cover your anxiety. Be
direct, warm, outgoing, and professional. If, because of the
nature of the material (e.g., a sitcom or comedy show) or the
circumstances of the audition, you feel the need to "charm
them up" and chitchat before you start reading, go to it. Sitcoms are personality-based. The auditors want to like you and

find you engaging, so they will often start a conversation as soon as you walk in the door.

Auditions are like other social situations. You don't want a friend who is trying too hard to be friendly, who wants desperately to please you, or who is forcing himself on you. Nor do you want a friend who is always intimidated by you.

One reason you may be feeling anxious is that when you walk into the audition area, you feel as though you are entering "their" space. You feel as though "they" control that space. You or your agent made the appointment with "them." You must wait for "them" to let you in. But, in reality, your auditors don't feel they own the space any more than you do. They may have rented the space for the day. Even if owned by a production company, your auditors as individuals don't own the space. The idea that the space is "theirs" diminishes you. Think of the area as a *work space* that belongs to you and your auditors. And if you give a great audition, you will feel as though *you* own it!

Try to enter the audition space with a feeling of ease. Michael Chekhov talked of a feeling of ease to release tensions and to give you a free flow of energy. Often actors tell themselves to relax when they feel tense or nervous. It's not quite the same. For me, there is a significant difference in the two ways of directing my body to behave. Relaxing makes me feel passive and sleepy; a feeling of ease gets rid of the stress in my body but maintains my alertness. Along with opening the body with the breath, it prepares the way for the pre-beat of the scene.

The misperception that your auditors are all-powerful may

make you feel physically small. You will feel more powerful in a physical as well as a psychological sense if you imagine that you have a greatly expanded presence. Acting teacher Dana Zeller-Alexis suggests that you imagine that your head touches the ceiling and your hands touch the walls: you fill the room. Use your good sense to tell you if this adjustment helps you. If it messes you up in terms of your character preparation, forget it. But it just might help you walk in the room.

READER

A twenty-one-year-old male reader may be playing your eighty-five-year-old grandmother. You never know in advance who the reader will be or how he will read the dialogue. My notion of a good reader is someone who understands the material and reads intelligently without imposing a strong personal point of view. The reader should leave you free to shape the material in any way you choose.

Casting directors are usually good readers. The opposite extreme is a reader who is an aspiring actor who may be trying to impress the auditors and acts too much, leading you in a direction in which you don't want to go. Or, you may have a reader who has been hired in a pinch and is practically illiterate. Or one who rushes through the material. (If the reader has the first line in the scene, and starts before you have indicated that you are ready, stop and say, "I need a moment.")

Actors feel terribly encumbered by a poor reader. My advice

is: *if the reader is poor, don't respond to the* WAY *the reader says the lines—respond to* WHAT *he is saying.* If you listen to the text rather than the interpretation, you can respond to the information in the scene in your own way. When you work on the material at home, imagine how the lines *should* be said so that you can respond according to your acting choices. Then, at your audition, respond to what you imagined, not to the reader. With practice you can manage it. Don't bring your acting down to the reader's level. Don't take on his rhythm, or feel the obligation to play the scene with him if he is way off the track. The auditors are looking and listening to *you*; they don't expect you to act with the reader unless it is clear the reader is someone with whom you can play the scene.

When the reader is poor, there is a tendency not to want to look at her because you find it distracting. Instead of listening, you look at the script while she is speaking. This is counterproductive. You will miss the continuity of the interchange. The auditors need to see your face as much as possible, and they want to watch you while you are listening.

In life, when we speak or listen to someone, our eyes shift frequently. However, to steady his nerves or to connect with the other character in the scene, an actor will often lock eyes with the reader. It is artificial and creates a very unnatural impression. Behave as naturally as possible, look at the reader when you need to and shift your eyes whenever it seems appropriate or you have the impulse to do so.

Sometimes there will be more than two characters in the

scene, but, typically, one reader reads all the other parts. The question arises, "Do I address all my lines to the reader, or do I speak to the reader as one character and turn away from the reader toward the other imaginary characters when they are speaking?" If you find it confusing to try to remember who else is speaking and where you have placed them when the only voice is coming from the reader, you can address all your lines to the reader. However, if you have time to become familiar with who is saying what and where, it serves a dramatic purpose to turn away to an imaginary character and then back to the reader. But be sure you make the reader the primary character you are addressing.

Keep a space between you and the reader. Its size should be determined by the nature of the scene and your relationship to the other character. If you are close to the reader for an intimate scene, be sure you leave a space between you so the auditors can see you. In creating intimacy, be sure not to drop your voice so low that they can't hear you.

An important note: if you decide you must touch the reader during your audition (although generally I don't think it's a good idea), be sure to ask her in advance. Also before you begin, tell your reader if you want her to jump in or delay coming in on a cue, etc. Keep your requests simple. Provided it doesn't take more than a minute or two, the auditors will wait until you're ready. You should prepare the instructions in advance so you can give them quickly and efficiently. And when you leave, it is gracious to thank the reader.

SCANNING TECHNIQUE

If you haven't had time to get familiar with the material, here is a technique that will help you during your audition. When you get to the last line of your speech, quickly scan down to the last few words of your partner's response (which is your cue) and the first few words of your next speech. This will enable you to look up from your script and listen to your partner's speech. You can get in the habit of scanning in this way. It just takes practice. When you rehearse for your audition, make a note of the moments at which it is most important that you not look at the script. You don't want to have to break an emotional or transitional moment by looking down at your script. *Learning how to be off the script even when you have not had much time to prepare, will improve your audition technique immeasurably.*

ACTING STAGE DIRECTIONS

If there is a stage direction that describes what the character is feeling, *(she cries hysterically, laughs uproariously; wipes away a tear)*, don't feel obliged to follow it mechanically. Regard the stage directions as a reflection of the author's point of view on the emotional state of the character. It is your choice whether to follow them. If you were playing the role, it would be up to you and the director to decide whether to follow the directions. But in an audition, consider the stage directions information that can help you make your actable choices.

"ANY QUESTIONS?"

You walk into an audition and are introduced to the director, who asks, "Do you have any questions before you begin?" You have had time to prepare, worked hard, made choices. You don't really feel you need to ask any questions before auditioning. But you think, "Maybe she would like to converse with me to see my natural, spontaneous behavior. Maybe she wants to lead me to some of her own choices. If I say no, will she think I'm cocky?" So, for the director's sake, you ask something rather insignificant about your character. The director responds to your insignificant question and goes on to tell you something quite different from your own take on the character. You then feel responsible for delivering the director's interpretation of the character on the spot. My advice is to do what you had prepared without asking any questions first. You're apt to give a better audition.

Some scenes, such as fragments of film or television scripts, where you need some missing vital information to make an intelligent choice, are inscrutable. In those cases, as I suggested earlier, try to find someone who can answer your questions in advance of the audition.

After you have read for the director, he may want to give you an adjustment. Listen carefully. Not all directors can express what they want you to do clearly or in acting terms, so you might need to decode the direction. If you don't fully understand his direction, don't be afraid to ask questions. If the director gives you several ideas, he is not going to expect you to incorporate all of them instantly. Do your best. He might just want to see if you can take direction, which means change some part of what you did on the spot.

CHAIRS

I have strong feelings about chairs. I think sitting tends to make you more passive than standing: it is harder to keep up your energy level. Rehearse at home standing and sitting and see if you don't feel more energy when you're standing. (For camera auditions, you usually sit, though you may have the option of standing and occasionally even moving around a bit.) Some actors feel more secure sitting if they're very nervous. They don't want to deal with the possibility of their legs shaking. You can always start sitting and then stand up, or vice versa. You are in control.

If you have decided to use a chair and there are none on the stage, ask for one. If you have the choice of a chair with or without arms, always choose the one without arms. You will have more freedom of movement. Don't ask, "Is it all right if I use a chair?" That immediately gives the auditor permission to decide rather than you. If the auditor has strong reasons for not wanting you to use a chair, he'll tell you. When the ball is in your court, keep it there.

POSITION

If you are auditioning in a large rehearsal room without a stage, be sure you keep a space of at least twelve to fifteen feet between you and the auditors. This will give you more freedom to move. The auditors need the space between you so they can get a perspective on your performance. Also if you are too close to them, they don't feel they can check your résumé if they need to, or confer with each other, for fear of distracting you. If you're very close, they feel assaulted! Even if you are in a small rehearsal room, do your best to create some distance between you and the auditors.

For theater auditions, you should take an upstage position, with the reader downstage and to the side. This gives the auditors an optimum view. You may find yourself moving downstage during the audition without being aware that you are playing most of the scene in profile. Not a good idea. When I was casting, I was frustrated if I rarely saw the actor's full face during the audition. You may be caught up in the scene and figure if doesn't matter. It matters. If we only see one quarter of your face or your profile during most of the audition, we can't get the full impact of your work. You are free to move, but you must be aware of your audience. If you were sitting in front of a camera for a film audition, would you turn away from the camera for the whole scene? You shouldn't do that on stage either.

A word about how to hold your script. An actor, in the heat of the moment, may hold his script in front of his face. Hold your script slightly off to the side, between your waist and shoulder. Find a comfortable angle that allows you to glance down without having to move your head too far to the side, or having to drop your head and raise it everytime you need to refer to the script. Practice reading scenes with an awareness of involuntary script movement. Don't disappear behind your script.

MOVEMENT

(He walks to the window and looks out at the garden.) That stage direction in the script doesn't require you to walk to a window and look out at the garden. It isn't necessary or even desirable to follow directions in the script to move from one place to another, unless it is essential to your acting choices. If the script calls for you to knock on the door, and it will help the dynamic of the scene, you can use your foot to simulate a knock. If you're playing a high-energy character, or one who is agitated or excited, you may feel you need to move. That's perfectly fine. There is no need to inhibit your movement. But don't feel obliged to obey the author's stage directions. Random pacing can dissipate your energy if it doesn't arise from your understanding of the character or the circumstances.

You may have a love scene in which there is a lot of hugging and kissing. You have a script in your hand. If you embrace your reader and then the two of you struggle to find your scripts, which end up behind each other's heads, it's very awkward for you to do and for us to watch. The auditors have read the script. They know where the hugs and kisses take place. You need to *experience* what's happening and respond to it, but there is no necessity to get all tangled up in arms and bodies and scripts. To establish a sense of intimacy between you and your reader, you might move closer, but that should suffice.

The same thing applies to fighting during a scene. You might want to mime a punch or slap because the power of the gesture helps your acting. That's okay if you're not too near the reader! But stamping the floor can also give you the sense of a violent gesture, and, because you're actually hitting something, it won't feel as fake to you or your auditors.

PROPS

If a stage direction in the script says "(*She picks up her glass and takes a sip*)," that doesn't mean you should bring a glass to your audition. It will likely be more of a hindrance than a help. What do you do with the glass when you have to turn the page? There's usually no table to put it on. If you are performing a staged monologue without a script, you might bring a prop or two. (Usually a table and chairs are provided for monologue auditions.) But, with that exception, bringing a prop to an audition seems amateurish. If you decide you *must* use something real, plan in advance what you're going to do with the prop when you're not using it or have to turn the page. Is it worth it?

COSTUME

Most actors know how to dress for an audition. They use their common sense. If you are going for an interview, wear something flattering and comfortable. Don't look as though you're going to a wedding.

If the audition is for a period piece, unless the text or character suggests otherwise, women shouldn't wear a mini-skirt or pants. A long skirt, or a midcalf length skirt, is a safe choice. For a period piece, men shouldn't wear jeans; a suit is usually appropriate. Try to wear the kind of shoes your character would wear.

If the audition is for a contemporary piece, you can suggest your character with a scarf, jeans, or a particular style of contemporary clothing. For women, your character usually dictates how light or heavy to go on your street makeup. However, it is not a good idea to wear a full costume to an audition. Like appearing without a script, it sets up an expectation among the auditors that they are going to see a performance. Daniel Swee, New York casting director for theater and film says, "Don't wear anything you wouldn't wear on the subway."

There are always exceptions to the rule. In the 1970s, before he had appeared in films, Kevin Kline auditioned for *On the Twentieth Century,* a Broadway musical directed by Hal

Prince. Kevin broke every rule. The show, written in farcical style, takes place in the 1920s. The characters are all overblown characters. Bruce Granit, Kevin's character, was a would-be Hollywood matinee idol: gorgeous, ambitious, stupid, and madly in love with himself. In the audition scene, his girlfriend, Lily Garland, a big movie star, boards a train to New York, having said goodbye to Granit. But Granit, at the last minute, follows her onto the train and tries to seduce her into letting him go to New York with her.

Kevin appeared at the preliminary audition wearing a white suit with a white overcoat draped over his shoulders, an outrageous tie, and a fedora jauntily perched on the back of his head. He carried no script. Our male stage manager read the role of Lily Garland (played by Madeline Kahn). Kevin swept onto the stage and performed the scene full-out, as though it were opening night. At one point he grabbed the stage manager and kissed him passionately on the mouth. Except for a blink and a gulp, the stage manager, being a pro, hardly missed a beat, straightened his glasses, turned the page, and went on playing the scene. Needless to say, Kevin got a callback, repeated his brilliant performance for Hal Prince, got the job, went on to win a Tony Award, and launched a successful career.

Kevin's audition became legendary. When he was about to leave the show, many actors who auditioned to replace him appeared in a fedora and a white suit with an overcoat draped over their shoulders. None of these actors could perform like Kevin. But they seemed more inadequate because of the expectations set up by the costume. Time and time again, as the incarnation of Bruce Granit walked onto the stage, we were disappointed. So, unless you're already as accomplished an actor as Kevin Kline, you're better off following my advice regarding costumes, holding scripts, and kissing readers.

LIGHT

Make sure you're in it. If you're auditioning on the stage of a large theater, chances are there will be a pool of light center stage, or a worklight (a naked light bulb on a stand) at the side of the stage. (The auditors would provide better lighting if it weren't so expensive, but in most large theaters you have to hire a union electrician to turn on any stage lights.)

Sometimes actors are nervous as they make their entrance, so they manage to get to a spot on the edge of the circle of light but no farther. They may be unaware that they are in partial darkness, or they may feel more comfortable not being in the light! In any event, paralysis seems to set in and they can't move. I hope by the time you finish this book, you will walk directly into the center of the pool of light, confident, filled with your own power, wanting to be seen.

VOLUME

If they can't hear you, they can't hire you. Adjust your volume according to the space in which you are auditioning. If you're auditioning for a Broadway production in an audition room, you don't have to project as though you were on a stage. Callbacks are sometimes held in the theater, in which case you must project accordingly.

Actors go back and forth from camera auditions to theater auditions in the same day. Be aware of the varying sound needs of each medium when you are rehearsing at home. If you have any doubt about the approximate size of the audition space, try to find out before you go. Otherwise, you may arrive at the audition and suddenly have to make a big adjustment. If you have to speak louder or softer than you had anticipated, it can throw you for a loop.

Michael Chekhov suggested that, when you need to speak loudly, think of radiating your voice, or sending it out. The desire to communicate words, thoughts, or feelings in the form of radiation will reach the place it needs to go without strain.

EXIT

Director Itamar Kubovy was auditioning actors for a play. An actor, after her audition, turned to Itamar and said, "Was I way off?" If Itamar really thought the actor was right for the role but "way off," he would have given her an adjustment at the time. Itamar either thought she wasn't right for the role, or didn't like her acting choices, or, perhaps he liked her work but wanted to wait until the end of the day to discuss all the actors who auditioned at the session with the other auditors. Don't put the director on the spot. You can try to get feedback from the casting director at a later time.

When you exit as the character in the scene, don't use the real door in the audition space. It's confusing to the auditors and awkward for you, as you may then have to reenter to pick up your things and end the audition properly. And if you don't reenter and let the auditors say thank you, they'll feel cheated! Try to leave whatever paraphernalia you've brought to the audition in a safe place in the reception room, or, if you want to bring it in with you, leave it near the door. Then, when you finish your scene, you can pick it up and leave gracefully.

If it takes too much time for you to leave, the postaudition exit can be a bit awkward, both for you and the auditors. They cannot speak to each other about your audition (or anything else) until you leave. If you've given a good audition, get out while the getting's good. And if you've given a poor audition, you will surely want to get out as quickly as you can.

CALLBACKS

If you are called back, you should feel more confident than you did at the preliminary audition. The director liked what you did. Nonetheless, I find that most actors don't feel more confident at the callback. On the contrary, because they realize they might actually get the job, the stakes are higher and they get anxious. What is expected at a callback? Basically, what you did at the first audition. You can deepen it, but don't try to improve it to the extent that your previous work is unrecognizable.

Yes—wear the same thing to the callback that you wore to the preliminary audition. Directors see a lot of actors and often identify them by what they wore, so why confuse them? "Let's see the one in the red dress." (Sorry, but they often will not remember your name.) The actor Debra Monk says, "Don't even bathe!"

CONCLUSION

Sometimes, unexpected situations come up at auditions. Rely on your judgment and common sense to figure out how to handle them. However, I hope that these suggestions will help you in creating the best possible scenario for your auditions.

Chapter IX

———■———

TIPS

In chapter VIII, I spoke about the practical issues involved in auditioning. Here are some miscellaneous thoughts, suggestions, and observations about your pre-audition state of mind, preparation for the audition, the audition itself, postaudition, callbacks, and feedback.

STATE OF MIND

Know thyself. Know what *you* need to give your best audition. Know how much time you need to prepare a scene and to feel confident that you have plumbed it for strong choices and can deliver a good audition. Don't give yourself excuses for not fulfilling those needs. Give every audition your best shot. That will improve your odds and will help the auditors decide to hire you.

Try to arrange your life so that you don't need the job you're auditioning for to pay last month's rent. And don't decide that this particular job will make your career. If you think that is the case, your subtext at the audition will be desperation. The last thing that auditors want to see or sense is a desperate actor. Most actors give better auditions when they don't have an enormous emotional investment in getting the job. The next time you have an audition at which you don't feel pressured and you audition well, check out your connection to your body and your way of working on the role. I think you'll find that you worked with a feeling of ease, without the kind of tension that inhibits access to your creative juices. Strive for that physical state of being at every audition.

Regard the audition as a valuable experience, apart from what may or may not come from it, not only as a means to an end.

Actors don't always realize that acting at an audition is still acting, even with a script in hand. Each moment leads to the next as it would in a performance. Play the action under the words. You still need to let your acting choices flow through you. You want to feel more true and less like you are reading lines. Be totally present. Your audition is a performance in the here and now.

PRE-AUDITION

Some scripts will strike you as prosaic or just awful. You might say, "Oh, the character is just like me" or "This scene is simplistic." You read it once or twice, then blow it off. If you decide to audition for the part, that's not a good idea! There's always something you can find in the script that will flesh out relationships, character, objectives, etc., and bring it to life.

On the flip side, when you're rehearsing an audition scene you are interested in, you may tend to work intensely and non-stop. Be sure to take frequent breaks. You will come back to the material each time with a fresher perspective. Whenever you prepare a role, whether for an audition or for a performance, the scene is developing in your subconscious as well as your conscious mind. You want to take advantage of that resource by giving yourself the time to process your work.

If you're preparing to audition for the part of a character whose point of view or behavior you don't like or don't approve of, don't "comment" on the character. Don't try to let the auditors know that you are unlike the character. Don't make fun of the character, even unwittingly. Play the character as you would any other, fully and truthfully, within the world of the play. Otherwise you will undermine your audition.

It is important to try to find one thing about the character you like, no matter how horrible or distasteful he may be. You cannot identify with a character about whom you have only negative feelings.

A casting director may call you in after not having seen you for any role for many years. She may be uncertain if you're right for the role she's casting, but she remembers she liked your work and wants to give you a shot at this job. Although it may be an exercise in hope rather than judgment on her part, take the opportunity to be seen again even if you feel the part is not for you. The audition may lead to something else down the road that is closer to your range and your talents.

Once you have become familiar with the script, try seeing the world through your character's eyes. You might notice a dress or jacket in a store window that your character might wear or not; either way, it will help you tune in to the way your character thinks and feels. You might experience a particular landscape, a park or city street, through the eyes of your character. You might pass a restaurant and wonder whether it is the kind of place your character would frequent, and, if not, what might be to her taste. Particular colors might or might not appeal to your character. Other people you pass might be of interest or not to your character. This exercise is a way of tuning in to and connecting in a playful and provocative way with your character. Do it on your way to the audition. It will bring you into your character's world.

AT THE AUDITION

Whether you've done a little or a lot of preparation, you should enter the audition space feeling enthusiastic about acting the role. The auditors are your audience. Their eagerness to cast the role should give you additional energy.

The director relies on the casting director to bring actors to the audition who are appropriate for the particular role being cast. Casting directors are at risk in granting you an audition, particularly if you have not been prescreened for the role. They put themselves on the line on your behalf. They hope their instincts are right and that you will connect with the role. When you walk into the room or onto the stage, remember that the casting director is always in your corner, rooting for you.

Don't try to watch yourself from the point of view of the auditors. It will prevent you from being open and available to whatever your choices and impulses may be. You will not be in the moment. Let the others watch you; get yourself in the scene and stay there!

Auditors can sense whether you're tense and suffering through an audition or at ease and enjoying the work. If *you* enjoy the audition, the auditors will be more likely to enjoy it. Don't work too hard. Or at least, don't look like you're working too hard.

Don't ask for the dates of callbacks or dates of the production at the audition. It sounds presumptuous, as though you're expecting to get the callback or the job and must clear your calendar. If you think you may have a conflict, ask the casting office or your agent for the callback dates or the production date *before* the audition.

If you ask a question or have a conversation with your auditors, speak to them as peers, not as judges.

Because you don't have the support system you have when you're performing, you may find it harder to commit to your acting choices at the audition. You don't have the director's input or any interaction with the other actors. You lose heart and doubt your acting choices. As result, you only do a small part of what you had intended to do. You play it safe. Try to be aware when self-doubt creeps up on you. Awareness of this tendency may help you to overcome it. Trust yourself.

If you miss a moment or two at your audition, don't look back. Ballet dancers often make errors—for example, in coming out of a turn, or making a wrong move—but they go on as though it didn't happen. How many champion ice skaters have you seen flop down on the ice, get up and continue their routines without missing a beat? I always look for an expression that reflects their disappointment or frustration, but I rarely see it. They keep a brave front and move forward to the next moment. It's important to realize that if you miss some of your choices or moments at the audition, it's not a disaster as long as you maintain your energy and focus.

You may go into an autopilot mode. You hear yourself saying the lines, but you're not there. You need to connect with your body and with the truth of the scene. Hold on to a chair to feel something palpable. If one is not readily available, feel the floor through your feet. That may help ground you literally and figuratively. Breathing can come to your rescue. (See page 168). When you breathe a sensation of openness into your body, you can feel it connect in a natural way. Exhale openness into the space around you. It will reconnect you with the room. It takes approximately one to two seconds to inhale and exhale. You can do it while you're listening to the reader. Become familiar with this process and use it at different times so it does not require your primary focus.

If nerves kick in, concentration goes out, and you've stopped breathing below your neck, remember why you are there. Nobody forced you to come to this audition. It is your choice. *You came because this is your work as an actor. You are there because you want to act.*

POSTAUDITION

Sometimes there is almost no way to give a good audition. If the material is poorly written, if the reader is bad, if the atmosphere seems negative, if you're given an impossible adjustment, etc., you can only give it your best and congratulate yourself on getting through it.

Auditions seem to happen very quickly, especially an audition that doesn't go well. You're in the audition space, you do your thing, you leave and it's over. There you are, out on the street, trying to remember exactly what you did, or didn't do, or should have done. Don't spend the day sulking or beating up on yourself. Go to the gym. Call a friend. Don't indulge in self-flagellation. Later you can evaluate the experience.

The good news is that you are often mistaken about the auditor's reaction. When auditioning, you are in the middle of the experience and cannot possibly have the point of view of the director. Any actor who auditions a lot will tell you she has often been surprised to get a callback or land a role, because she thought her audition was terrible.

Sometimes you won't know if you're going to be called back, or whether you are being seriously considered for a role, for weeks at a time. Your desire to play a particular role sticks to your ribs, your psyche, your heart. Let it go. It's just one audition. There will be many more in the course of your career. You did your work. Now forget about it. On to the next. If you get the job, that's great. But don't carry it around with you, letting it stew and driving you nuts.

CALLBACKS

The atmosphere at the callback will rarely be the same as it was at the preliminary audition. It may be in a different place. There will probably be more auditors. And your own emotional investment, as I suggested earlier, will be greater. It won't feel the same as the preliminary audition. Expect a difference. Otherwise, you may be thrown off track.

I had an experience at a callback that taught me a lesson. The project was a television movie. I read two scenes at the preliminary audition for the casting director alone. I knew that the producers would be at the callback. Two of them were young friends with whom I had worked twelve years earlier in a producer's office for an extended period of time. I hadn't seen them or been in touch with them since. Knowing they would be there made me apprehensive. (I always prefer to audition for strangers.) I walked into the audition room: a sound studio, with a camera, lights, and six people sitting at a table. My two friends leapt up and embraced me. We screamed and hollered that we all looked the same. I was then introduced to the other producers. I sat down in front of the camera and everybody became very quiet. They asked if I was ready and I said, "I need a moment." I tried to quiet myself after all the greetings and chit chat, and get into the character's space. I confess I had not prepared a pre-beat because I had slipped easily into the scene at the preliminary.

I was caught short. I read the first scene self-consciously, half of me resonating from the screaming and hollering, and the other half trying to connect with the scene. By the second scene, I had warmed up a bit, but not enough to make up for blowing the first scene.

With hindsight, I know I should have come into the room, said hello to my friends, and then suggested we talk later. My focus would have been preserved and they would have gotten the message. *You can never count on auditors to protect your audition. That's up to you.*

FEEDBACK

Your agent (if you have one) will usually call the casting director after your audition to find out if you are in the running and how you fared. If the auditors think you gave a very good audition, your agent will pass that along to you. If you don't hear anything from your agent or the casting director after an audition, you should know that asking for feedback is risky.

A young actor I know asked her agent for feedback after an audition. The agent called her back and said, "The casting director says you're not pretty enough." The agent, if not the casting director, should have known better. That comment could destroy any confidence the actor has in her looks. Can the actor be prettier for her next audition? Comments like that sink into your consciousness and are hard to forget. ("Branded in my brain" is how one of my students expressed it.)

God knows, women, and particularly female actors, in the United States are confronted with a conventional standard of beauty every day of their lives. This is also true for young leading men. Actors know that, in many roles, particularly for film and television, looks and not talent can be a major issue. When the agent told his client she wasn't pretty enough, did he expect her to say, "Oh, I'm glad to know that, I was afraid she didn't like my acting?" Not bloody likely. How many actors can be objective about such a comment?

Actors must present themselves confidently time and time again to gain employment. Their agents should appreciate the importance of passing along comments that are constructive and keeping their mouths shut about the rest. Most agents are sensitive enough to protect their clients from feedback that serves no purpose other than making them feel bad about themselves.

Actors want to learn and improve. They welcome feedback

that is instructive or informative, even though it may be hard to take. A director's feedback (via the casting director) is often responsive only to whether the actor is right for the role. The director doesn't usually focus on the details of the actor's audition. The casting director is more likely to notice, because she relies on her observations for future casting. Some casting directors are able to pinpoint what didn't work in the audition. That might help you do better in future auditions.

In some cases (usually for television shows), there is a huge casting rush and there isn't time for the casting director to do anything but get the show cast. The most common response to your agent's request for feedback (if he can get her on the phone in between sessions) is, "The director decided to go another way." This is a general comment that lets you know the job is not going to happen and the casting director doesn't have time to deal with the details of your audition.

It's up to you whether you want to rely on your own evaluation of your audition or ask for feedback if it is not forthcoming.

Chapter X

———◼———

A LITTLE ADVICE FROM

SOME EXPERTS

I asked a few colleagues what advice they would like to pass on to actors who audition. We all don't agree on everything. Make up your own mind. Here is what they said (in alphabetical order).

"Familiarize yourself with the material and how it might relate to you. Don't second-guess me and arrive in costume and with a bag full of props. I'm interested in your personality and how it might jell with my sense of the role. But my mind isn't set—it will change as actors show me things I would never have thought of. For me, auditions are an invaluable part of the process of discovery. When we read, I'll always ask for different choices even if I like what I get the first time. I want to test our ability to communicate with each other and the actor's skill in making adjustments."

—Michael Apted, film director

"Directors and producers are sometimes not sure exactly what they are looking for. You can help them by going in to the audition with confidence, and presenting them with your best interpretation of the character. It is helpful to briefly discuss what you think of the script and the character, and to convey your passion for the project before you read the scene."

—Joan Chen, actor and film director

"Relax. Do what you came to do. And if they don't take you, it's their loss."

—Keith David, actor

"Don't fake it, be true. Take chances, dare to fail. And keep me awake!"

—Gordon Davidson, director, artistic director, producer

"Auditioning: the difficult part is surviving the industry, which is a culture of rejection. Facing that in the most courageous manner, I rely on a quote from Winston Churchill, 'True power is an individual's ability to move from failure to failure with no loss of enthusiasm.' "

—Bill Duke, actor, film director, producer

"There is no one else who will give *your* audition. I repeat, no one!"

—Scott Ellis, director

"1) I like it when the actor has read the entire script, not just the part he or she is auditioning for.

2) And I like it when the actor comes in having given some thought to the part. Sometimes actors even dress for roles, and I appreciate that.

3) Sometimes an actor is brought in to read for a role, and afterwards suggests he be able to read for another role instead. I like this, too.

4) I can't tell you how many times I have cast actors for parts they did not come in for. I always keep a list of people I've liked and then, toward the end of casting a movie, I go through it and try to find some sort of part for each of them, even if it's only as a day player. So actors should keep in mind that a working director will often remember an audition either for other parts in the same project or for subsequent projects.

5) Sometimes an actor will come in and change the lines of the part he or she is auditioning for. Usually, I don't like this. I mean, a certain amount of changing is acceptable—especially after they've gotten the part—but part of the function of an audition is to hear the script, and it's hard to hear it if someone fools around with it. This is a particularly tricky thing to do, by the way, if the writer is sitting in on the audition. (On the other hand, I have cast actors who have changed lines, especially when what they did was funnier than what was written. But this is rare.)

6) An actress who wanted to be in one of my movies sent me

some brownies. They were the most delicious brownies I have ever had in my life. You can't imagine how great they were. I realized that I would have to cast her in the movie because otherwise she would never give me the brownie recipe. But I read her, and she really wasn't right for the movie. So I didn't cast her. She did, however, give me the brownie recipe. But the point I want to make here is that in the end, no matter what an actor does in the way of charming and ingratiating things, in the end it's the acting ability that counts."

—Nora Ephron, screenwriter and director

"Sitting in on auditions with David Kelley, I was amazed by two things: how little actors had prepared, believing, I think, that they should make a general choice and not make any impositions on the material. And how everyone in the room genuinely hoped the next actor would assume control of the room and be 'it.'

Believe they are looking for you. Believe that the reason they are having you read is because they are hoping you are about to make their day shorter, that you are what they have been looking for.

Bring in a little piece of you. A little secret, a little something you like about yourself. The hardest thing for an actor to believe is that we are enough, but we are.

They will not come to you. You must make an offer and it should be an offer you like and can support."

—Jessalyn Gilsig, actor

"The best advice anyone gave me about auditioning that I carry with me to this day is that an audition is always about the work and nothing else. For me, that means not trying to please anyone but myself. I set out to do my job and that's that. I also like to think of an audition like a one-person show that opens and closes in one performance. After the audition, I try my best not to get crazed about feedback. If they want me for the job, they'll hire me.

I'm not very social at auditions. I find that I must stay focused and quiet. I usually try to find a space away from the waiting room and let the receptionist know where I am.

I try to have fun in my auditions.

I try to have the lines memorized or at least be very familiar with them. I have the most freedom to play that way."

—Lisa Gay Hamiton, actor

"It never helps an actor's case when he or she begins an audition by apologizing. Frankly, the fact that you just picked up the sides or that you were sick last night and couldn't study them—we forget extenuating circumstances once you get about three lines into the audition scene, and end up judging whatever you present to us. Moreover, explaining away what you expect to be a less-than-first-rate reading gives a bad first impression, making you appear less-than-first rate. An exception may be in musical auditions, if your singing voice is ailing due to a cold or other illness. In most cases, however, it's best to give 100 percent of whatever you've got—in which case, we will end up with no idea that you just had your tonsils out yesterday,"

—David Henry Hwang, playwright and screenwriter

"If I am auditioning for the part of a character named Rita, I always say to myself, 'Rita couldn't be here today, so I will do her part.' It makes me feel like I'm doing them a favor and they know it. Kind of stupid, but it works.

Instead of dreading the audition, it's good to remind yourself that acting is what you love to do, and you get to act! So rather than hearing yourself say, 'Ugh, I have an audition today,' say 'I get to act today!'

Bring fear with you. Own it and use it."

—Allison Janney, actor

"Actors don't make an impression on me without making strong choices. There's no one answer or choice I'm looking for, and that should be liberating because it gives the actor many options."

—James Lapine, playwright, screenwriter, director

"Auditioning is an art unto itself. And, unfortunately, many of us are never taught this art form. There are so many variables that make up a good audition. Being prepared, being relaxed, owning the material, feeling comfortable in your skin, the ability to have a dialogue about the script, being flexible enough to take direction, and being yourself in this most unusual circumstance. But the one thing I know for certain is that the person with the most confidence wins.

In the beginning of my career, I spent years being a reader for auditions. And I was constantly stunned at how roles were cast. It was not always the best actor, the most obvious person. It was, however, the person who commanded the room, demanded our attention, insisted (in a very subtle way) that we take them seriously. Those men and women are the ones who won out time after time, year after year. Confidence is key. Not to be confused with apathy, but to be worn like a favorite pair of faded jeans that you slip into for comfort.

And if you are like most people and you aren't filled to the brim with confidence, you must *act* like you are. In fact, that is the biggest acting challenge of all in an audition. And once you start pretending to be confident, you will reap the rewards of its power. And real confidence will soon take its place. It all just builds on itself.

Self-acceptance begets acceptance from others, which begets even deeper, more genuine self-acceptance. It can be done. But no one is going to bestow it on you. It is a gift only you can give yourself."

—Camryn Manheim, actor

"I think of auditions as small performances: the actor is giving me a glimpse of how he or she might approach the role. What most excites me is the actor who brings him or herself into the room, and allows the reading to incorporate his or her own personality into the role. That way I'm not watching someone become a chameleon so much as really getting a strong sense of how the actor as a person intersects with the character. When the actor tries to 'disappear' into the role at an audition, the actor really does disappear, and it's that much harder for me to enter the performance."

—Michael Mayer, director

"You are required to be optimists because as actors, you will deal with a lot of shit, and it is the optimist's job to turn shit into gold."

—Michael Miller, artistic director

"When I was a young actor in London doing mostly film and television, a friend encouraged me to audition for a Shakespeare play that Peter Hall was directing. I wasn't interested in the job and I didn't know how to do Shakespeare but my friend, who was also a director, persisted. He offered to work with me on two monologues from Shakespeare which would show my range.

When I arrived, an assistant told me that Peter Hall had a lunch date and that he would only have time to hear one monologue. I began the first monologue but stopped in the middle and said, 'Mr. Hall, I can only do these two monologues together, so you just go to your lunch date.' I prepared to leave and Peter Hall came running down the aisle and offered me the job.

What I learned from this experience is that an actor must find a reason not to care whether he gets the job or not. You will always do your best work.

When I'm auditioning actors for a play that I'm directing, I like the actors to know the material cold. That way I know they've made choices. However, they should always hold the script and make a pretense of looking at it, even if they don't need to refer to it."

—Brian Murray, actor and director

"One common mistake I find many actors make is overworking a scene so that they are trapped by the time they come in to the audition. They can only do the scene one way. You have to be open and prepared to mix it up. I often change a character's objective in a scene just to see if the actor can take direction. If they can't, I take it as a sign of a weak actor."

—Gina Prince-Bythewood, film director

"I caution all auditionees: don't try to anticipate me or give me what you think I want. You will invariably be wrong and obscure what I do want. I want to see you fully: your thinking, your full impulse. From that, I might see something that I can use to get what I want.

And remember that more parts are lost in the walk from the wings to center stage than are lost at center stage."

—Lloyd Richards, artistic director

"I don't want auditions to be a test. If the actor is interesting and talented, but isn't right for this, I may use him or her in something else."

—John Sayles, actor, screenwriter, director, producer

"On a high-self-esteem day, I think how lucky they are that I'm there to show them all my best stuff."

—Kyra Sedgwick, actor

"Prepare the material carefully so that it represents your talent, and don't take the results too seriously, especially if you get the job."

—Ed Sherin, director and producer

"Forget the whole notion of 'type.' 'Type' is a mutable, subjective idea, and one that the actor has no control over. 'Type' is limiting. As long as you have a realistic sense of who you are and how you are likely to be cast—let others decide, if they need to, what 'type' you are.

Don't try and figure out what 'we' are looking for. All the clues you need are in the text. Now it's up to you to create a character based on that information. Do your homework, and then go for it!

Breathe."

—Meg Simon, casting director

"As for advice, I would only echo one of David Craig's principles: the audition starts the minute you walk onstage or into the rehearsal room. How you conduct yourself before you open your mouth is as important as anything that happens afterwards. This includes not having an attitude (e.g., being either too intense or overeffusive), what you wear, etc."

—Stephen Sondheim, composer, lyricist, playwright, screenwriter

"If there is only one thing you can remember before coming into an audition, it should be to know that the people in the room want you to be as good as you are. Before each actor walks into the room, we are hoping that he or she will get cast."

—Bernard Telsey, casting director

"Here's my audition tip. Never bring a prop, never try to be funny, and never do a striptease. The latter gets very scary."

—Wendy Wasserstein, playwright and screenwriter

"The most important thing an actor can do in an audition is to relax. In a relaxed state, not only does an actor's talent shine through, but so does their intelligence and humor.

How an actor treats the audition pianist is a true sign of what their rehearsal behavior will be like with their fellow actors. If they are rude, condescending or unnecessarily aggressive to the pianist, I take that as a warning sign."

—George C. Wolfe, playwright, director, producer, artistic director

"I find it extremely gratifying to prepare exhaustively, which can be a tremendous confidence booster. I have, by this time, a very thorough drill, a preparation routine which I have developed through trial and error and getting to know myself and my weaknesses. I find it to be very dependable and it demystifies the unpleasantness of it all."

—B. D. Wong, actor

Chapter XI

———————

THE CARE AND FEEDING

OF AN ACTOR

This is the Jewish Mother part. A little advice for your own good that goes beyond auditioning or an acting career. Let's talk about your life as an actor. You have some choice in the matter.

A CAREER IN ACTING?

In October, 1998, Bill Bradley was asked if he thought he would run for president. He said that when he considered that option, he asked himself the question, Does my ability match the moment?

How do you know if your "ability matches the moment," i.e., whether you have the talent and "castability" to have a decent shot at a career in the acting profession? If you have had the opportunity to develop your skills as an actor, auditioned a lot and not been hired, rarely been called back, and hardly ever received encouragement from anyone but friends or teachers you pay, you need to get real about your chances. How much of your life are you willing to spend trying to do something that is so competitive that only a small percentage of professionals work regularly enough to support themselves?

HARD TIMES

Show business can bruise and batter the most talented actors, even those who have "successful" careers in the profession. The rule rather than the exception is that they don't work for months at a time. They audition and often are not hired. While they wait for the next job, they get sucked into the desperation that often accompanies unemployment. They lose touch with their talent and with themselves as human beings. They become frustrated, cynical, and grim. Some leave the business. Others don't and stay frustrated and angry. Some go into therapy if they can afford it. How can you survive in this difficult profession?

WHAT TO DO

My advice is: If you decide on an acting career, whether or not you have a day job or can survive without one in between acting gigs, you need to be a self-initiator. *You need to take care of the actor within you in a conscious way. You need to nurture your talent. You need to use your down time to stretch your acting muscles and to continue to renew yourself as an actor and a human being.*

Here are some ways to be out of work creatively:

Take classes that will improve your skills Take a scene study class, a Shakespeare workshop, a clowning weekend, a camera workshop, a voice class, a class in improvisation or jazz dancing. If you can't afford to take a class, get together with some colleagues and read a play or script together on a regular basis. Work on different accents and dialects. You should be able to do an English, Irish, Southern, or New York accent at the drop of a hat. (Dialect tapes are available at bookstores that specialize in material for actors.)

Find mentors Find teachers, coaches, or other actors whom you trust, and who inspire you, from whom you can continue to learn or relearn.

Exercise Keep your body in good shape for your work as well as your health. You might get a job next week that requires you to do stage combat, or to fake a fight in an action film, or take a fall. You might get a part in a play that will require you to rehearse while performing eight times a week in previews, or a film that requires long days on the set. Your stamina will determine, in part, how well you are able to fulfill the requirements of your role. And it makes you look and feel better.

Stimulate your artistic sensibilities Go to the theater; if you can't afford a ticket, call and see if you can usher. Rent movies that have performances by actors you admire. Study their camera technique. Go to a museum and study paintings of different periods; they will supply you with images for plays or films. Listen to music that stirs you. Keep looking for inspiration that feeds your soul.

Don't let show business be the only thing in your life Show business tends to be insular. Actors spend a lot of time talking about it, complaining about it, trying to fathom it. Expand your horizons. Take classes in a foreign language, computers, or creative writing. Read books other than plays. Read the front page of the paper and not just the Arts section. Actors get so focused on themselves that they forget about what else is going on in the world.

Volunteer There are innumerable organizations and institutions that do good work and would value your help. Give of yourself. Be useful. You don't have to make a long-term commitment. You will feel fulfilled and gain a saner perspective on your life and your career. (Look up Social and Human Services in the Yellow Pages.)

Husband your time. Don't waste it Learn something every day, whether it relates to your work or not. All of it feeds you and will make you a better actor and a better person. Good act-

THE CARE AND FEEDING OF AN ACTOR

ing is not all talent and magic. If you want to continue to grow as an actor, you need to be conscientious and thoughtful about your life as well as your craft.

Relationships It's not easy for actors to have long-term relationships. Actors work odd hours. They travel. Their lives are unpredictable. They live on the edge. However, relationships are what most of us think life is all about. Don't take them for granted. Be sure that your partner, spouse, children, and/or friends are, along with your work, your highest priority.

Community One of the most wonderful perks you have as a working actor is a feeling of community. You feel it when you're in an acting program. You feel it when you're in the cast of a play, a film, a TV show, or in an ongoing company or series. One of the hardest things about being out of work is being alone and feeling isolated. You need a support system of friends, family, other actors, teachers, agents, managers, or all of the above. Classes will help connect you with other people in the acting community. Volunteering will connect you with a community outside your acting circle. Don't let yourself fall victim to the loneliness and self-doubt of unemployment. Whatever you do, don't suffer alone. And, maybe you won't suffer.

Know why you want to act. The reason may change as your career evolves, but stay in touch with it, whatever it is. It will serve as your own personal support system.

Without a conscious effort to maintain a healthy and productive life while you're not working, you may lose confidence in yourself as an actor and as a human being. And without self-confidence, you will not give a good audition.

CONCLUSION

Be philosophical about your career. Every actor has his or her own path. There are as many paths to success as there are successful working actors.

Bring the joy and the passion you feel as an actor to your auditions. Embrace the challenge. Embrace your power. You are the well. What you need is within you.

There is a constant and never-ending search for talent in our business. Talent can look like Danny DeVito, Gwyneth Paltrow, or Whoopi Goldberg. But it is always compelling for one reason or another. Whatever your talent, my friends, nourish it and develop it. If you do, someone out there will mine it and put you to work.